THE
BAKER'S SON
MY LIFE IN BUSINESS

THE
BAKER'S SON
MY LIFE IN BUSINESS

**THE STORY OF HOW THE
GOLDEN KRUST EMPIRE WAS
BUILT, FROM A VILLAGE SHOP
IN JAMAICA TO THE HEIGHTS OF
AMERICAN ENTERPRISE**

Lowell Hawthorne
with Michael A. Grant

Published by Akashic Books
©2012 by Lowell Hawthorne

Hardcover ISBN-13: 978-1-61775-125-7
Trade Paperback ISBN-13: 978-1-61775-124-0
Library of Congress Control Number: 2012932526

Akashic Books
PO Box 1456
New York, NY 10009
info@akashicbooks.com
www.akashicbooks.com

To the memory of my parents,
Mavis and Ephraim Hawthorne, whose Christian
values, unwavering faith, and iron-clad integrity
created a home environment in which our
family found love, a spirit of sharing, and a sense
of industry, laying the foundations on which our
success and that of the next generations could be built.
A percentage of the proceeds will go toward the
Mavis & Ephraim Hawthorne Golden Krust Foundation.

And we know that all things work together
for good to them that love God, to them who
are the called according to His purpose.
—Romans 8:28

CONTENTS

ACKNOWLEDGMENTS

My journey to the completion of this memoir has taken me back and forth to Jamaica more times than I can count. Over a five-year period, I've made notes, sat through and conducted interviews, and unearthed documents and photographs that have given shape to key events and memories I may otherwise have lost. Thanks be to God, I had the help of a cooperative family, friends, and associates who helped fill in the gaps of a story that is at once mine, that of my family, and, of course, about Golden Krust. The idea for *The Baker's Son* emerged while my father, Ephraim Hawthorne, was still alive and active as a consultant and confidant, so I thank him for his counsel and my late mother, Mavis Hawthorne, for her inspiration.

My wife Lorna, children Daren, Monique, Omar, and Haywood—whom I thank for their guiding principles—were first in line to contribute their opinions and recollections. I'm grateful to them for the compassion and detail they have lent to this project. Also instrumental with their input were other members of the Hawthorne clan, as well the wider Golden Krust family. My sister, Lauris "Mother" Hawthorne, who gave me her unconditional love and extended to me the opportunity to come to the U.S. for my life-changing experience, was an early collaborator. I thank her with all my heart.

Kellie Magnus, Linney Smith, Pauline Bennett O'Leary, Pat Rogers, Candice Richards, Bossville Rhoden, Karen Miller Levy, Juliet Young, Monica Campbell, Stephen Hill, and Sharon Whyte, Robert Hill, and Robert Gretczko were valuable readers and advisors. Herma Hawthorne showed wonderful patience and intuition in reading the manuscript and advising me on the best approach and process for telling my life story.

Special thanks to Derek Dingle, senior vice president and editor-in-chief of *Black Enterprise*, for suggesting that my life should be captured in a book. He lit the fire during the weeks he took notes.

In the last six years, I've learned more about myself than I ever had before. This is true because of Michael Grant. He has traveled with me throughout Jamaica, watched me deliver mini-sermons, observed my management meetings, was there to applaud when I made scholarship presentations at my alma mater, and ate with me on several occasions at my private residences. He has also played an integral role in the development of some of Golden Krust's branding and product packaging. Michael has invested many hours getting to know my immediate family, my siblings, close friends, former bosses, and even teachers from my early childhood. The composition of this biography would not have been possible without his unique writing skills, his insatiable quest for details, and most important, his passion to accurately tell the Golden Krust story. It was not an easy journey, but draft after draft, and despite several new twists and turns along the way, both in my personal and professional lives, he remained committed to capturing the life's journey which has been such a pleasure to recount. I extend heartfelt thanks to Michael and the team at Great House for the countless days and nights put into accomplishing this amazing milestone.

Any life of even moderate success depends on the kindness and tolerance of others—usually one's relatives or people who are just as close. For priceless contributions to my life in general, I would also like to recognize my mother-in-law Hyacinth (Mammy) and her husband Harvey for being like parents to me; my stepmother Phyllis, Auntie Paulette, and John Brown (Neville); Velma, a true champion from the beginning; my sister-in-law Janice and my brother-in-law Vincent; my brother-in-law Kevin Lee and sister-in-law Monica Dennis Hawthorne; my ten brothers and sisters—Cassandra, Lorraine, Jacqueline, Novelet, Lauris, Lloyd, Charles, Leroy, Raymond, and Milton; my nieces and nephews; my church family, including Pastor Leroy Richards who prays with me constantly; Dr. Sam Vassel; my mentor Alfred Simms; my accountant Winston Thompson; attorney Michael Aspinal and my legal team; my adopted brother Stanley Dennis; my niece Desrene, one of my unsung heroines and my inspiration.

I give thanks for the directors of the Golden Krust board Vincent, Scott, Alfred, and Marc. To my friend Dr. Hector Estepan, I give my gratitude for ensuring that I stay healthy. Special thanks to Godfrey Wallace, who solved the puzzle and came up with the name *Golden Krust*.

Finally, I have undying appreciation for Kai Ng, Al Alston, Garnett "Byron" Morrison, Burnett "Garvey" Morrison, Earl Chin, David O'Brien, Sergeant Marty Turetsky (NYPD Ret'd.), Earl Jarrett, Ms. Thelma James, and, of course, the Golden Krust team, the management and corporate staff, our valued franchisees, the bakeries and restaurants staff, and the brave founding members of Golden Krust, upon whose shoulders I stand.

INTRODUCTION

I can hardly wait to get to work each morning, especially after all that brainstorming in my head the night before. Despite my preoccupation with work, however, I am very involved in the lives of my wife, children, and the wider family with a routine that includes being home for dinner and at church on Sunday.

This ability to keep my mind running on parallel tracks was developed early in life as a young entrepreneur. Those early days of uncertainty, brought on by the fear that my fledgling business might not make it through another week, taught me how to juggle many balls at the same time.

Despite being the founding president and CEO of Golden Krust Caribbean Bakery, America's foremost Caribbean brand, and one of the top black-owned family businesses in the country, I never head straight for my private office on a typical morning. Purely by habit, my day usually begins with a tour of the machine shop or the bakery, where I walk among the giant stainless steel mixers, dough sheeters, and meat kettles that churn out our products. These are the tools of a trade that has consumed my family for most of our lives, and I look forward to the sense of grounding and tradition that I feel when I am in the plant. As always, the guys are ready with a quick hello as I greet each one like additional members of my already large family. We know each other the way a football team does: everyone with a serious role, but comfortable enough with teammates in the midst of serious business.

Although our principal manufacturing facility covers most of a city block, there is no designated parking space for my car. The managers and factory team all know that the production targets take priority, and so vehicles and trailers have their pick of available spots along the building. As a result, there are often vehicles blocking my way to a parking spot when I arrive.

One such morning is forever etched in my memory. It was a chilly Tuesday in March 2007. I noticed that the snow from the week before had started to melt, but there was still enough white on the ground to make a sunny morning sparkle even more brightly. The crunchy ice underfoot threatened my usual quick step as I made my way toward the plant entrance. I'm always anxious to get started.

I found things humming along normally at our Park Avenue (Bronx, New York) manufacturing plant. Work crews tended to the truck fleet lining our sidewalk; forklifts ran nonchalantly back and forth in the loading area.

While I had done this routine thousands of times before, I recall a heightened sense of anticipation that day. One reason was that we were in the midst of a changeover to a new process for our seasonal product, Easter buns. Another was the installation of our new automated high-capacity line, purchased in Europe, for making Jamaican patties.

Production of Jamaican patties, our signature product, would have to be halted temporarily while the kinks got worked out of the new process in the coming days. So depending on the version of the product we were committed to that week, whether baked or unbaked, meat-filled or not, the logistics of storage, refrigeration, and displaced capacity had to be sorted out.

Each year, the first hint of spring signals the start of our busy Easter production cycle. By ten a.m. during this period, hundreds of thousands of products might have already left the dock, several problems could have been solved, and perhaps even one or two disasters averted. This is when our production lines really hum, cranking out a minimum run of one hundred thousand spice buns. A derivative of the old British dessert tradition, the product sells rapidly through the Golden Krust franchise system and other outlets. West Indians, particularly Jamaicans and loyal devotees of Jamaican food, begin the hunt for Easter buns by late March. Because of religious observances, many Jamaicans take a break from eating meat (except for fish) during Easter, so the aromatic buns and their sweet symphony of fruit, allspice, anise, cinnamon, nutmeg, and rosewater take over the senses at that time of year. Once folks acquire their supply, they proceed to empty the neighborhood grocery stores of the cheese that's so important between slices of this traditional Easter treat. And since it was almost Easter, I also wanted to be sure that the bun-making tradition established by my father, Ephraim, was still alive and well. I had to make sure that the recipe he brought from the hills of St. Andrew in Jamaica still made the same great product we put out in the early days of Golden Krust.

There I was, picking my way through the maze of pallets and bakery racks bound for the main ovens. I had to taste the first buns made ready for quality testing. Even before sampling, I sensed a serious problem. The first batch of buns didn't have Papa's lovely brown crust and the aroma he coaxed out with his molasses and secret ingredients. To make matters worse, the flavor wasn't quite right, either. I was in deep trouble . . .

CHAPTER ONE
My Papa

I spent a long time recalling the spicy aroma, taste, and consistency of the Jamaican Easter buns we had baked back home, comparing them to the bun I first tasted that morning. Then I thought of Papa, the recognized expert in the baking of classic Easter buns. I felt instantly overwhelmed. Sure, I grew up watching, listening, and tasting, but never really knew the secrets of his recipe. That had always been his territory, a place I never thought I'd need to go—especially not so soon. He had always stressed the importance of consistency and went to great lengths to recapture the taste-memory that his customers carried from their own childhoods. Even now, we still place the highest value on the production techniques he developed in the early days, and it's for this reason that our bun-production equipment still includes some unique components fabricated in Jamaica.

My anxiety mounted as I asked myself: *What would Papa do to make the buns just right?* Perhaps he would have adjusted the mix or the caramelization. For sure, he would not stop trying until he perfected it. I comforted myself with the thought that I had watched him so keenly over the years. At this critical moment, I could only transport my mind back to the time I stood by Papa's side as he measured and mixed and perfected the Easter dough, and I hoped for the best results. So much depended on my protecting the family tradition and Papa's reputation as a baker that I couldn't afford to fail.

Another thought reminded me of how much Papa's presence still dominated the factory floor. There, next to the oven, was a single empty chair, a modest plastic seat like the kind you'd find in a public school classroom. It was one of the actual chairs my dad always used to sit on when he came up from Jamaica to visit. As close as I had been to him, I didn't think of making the symbolic gesture in his honor. Like clockwork, the bakers on duty put out a chair in exactly the same spot where he always sat at Eastertime.

He would visit us each year just before the spring, when it should still be too cold for an old man from the tropics. The warmth of that dark, isolated spot must have given him comfort from the chill outside. I imagine it was also his way of isolating himself from the main activity in the plant, closing himself off from all the other goings-on in favor of his beloved Easter bun production. After all, some of the guys at the plant had worked for Papa back in Jamaica and had taken orders from him there. This was Easter; they had always known instinctively who to listen to at this time of year. This season, all we had in the plant was his chair, and I was on the spot.

Papa was the one who was always ready with calm, wise advice, and he exuded the kind of humility that is not common in men who successfully combine the roles of respected church elder, successful businessman, and family patriarch. I revered Papa so much that I had been ready to name the company in his honor when we were starting out. Our first vehicles had even carried the "Hawthorne & Sons" name despite the fact that our U.S. corporation had no legal connection with the old business in Jamaica.

Always the boss, my father could easily have played that accustomed role whenever he made the annual trip to New York. But he didn't. He happily climbed into the role of Papa, joking with the guys, watching intently, and spending most of his time sitting by the oven. It's strange to think of it now, but even before the Golden Krust brand reached its unprecedented heights in the new millennium, Ephraim Hawthorne could have had any place of honor he desired. But for the asking, he could have been chairman of the board, or had his own executive suite at Golden Krust headquarters with a stretch limousine at his disposal. Anything. He simply preferred to be close to what had started in my sister's basement many years before—the baking of the beloved Easter bun.

Papa's quality-assurance routine was simple. He would touch a raw loaf as it traveled to the proof box for fermentation. If the sample was off-standard, he would simply send the batch back. Later, when the first racks of fresh buns emerged, they were cued up right there at his spot, next to a machine housing that also doubled as a makeshift desk and lunch table. Then he would get up—a little more slowly once he started relying on his cane for support—and perform his touch-and-taste test. If they were perfect, he would tap the rack with the walking stick and say, "This one's okay. This can go out, man," or pat a fresh unit with his hand and grandly declare, "Smooth as a baby's bottom!"

But he was not there this time to reject the batch or tell the guys what to do. He wouldn't be testing the buns and he wasn't coming to sit in that chair. So I did what I had seen him do so many times before: I assigned quantities and measures of ingredients in my head for each adjustment. Then I got to work, personally milling the first thousand pounds of dough for the production run. That's the beauty of mass production. If you can make a big enough batch that's perfect, then the quality of your production run is assured—unless you can afford to risk a few thousand pounds of flour for a little experiment. By the time I had decided to take action that morning, we had already condemned more than a thousand buns. After several heart-throbbing hits and misses, we finally came close to Pop's formula!

The Easter buns of 2007 turned out true to Golden Krust standards, and were once again a hit with our customers. We had restored the heights of bun-making Papa had established and for which our bakery had become famous.

On the day I rescued our batch of Easter buns, my father had been gone for almost a year. His sudden death was very difficult for me, and for several weeks I found it almost impossible to focus on anything but his memory. Papa was my confidant and mentor, master baker, counselor, and, of course, family pastor. The monuments to his memory now range from an effective nonprofit foundation to an informal wall shrine in my sister Lorraine's office, but that Tuesday morning was the first time that his absence had such a profound impact on me. It meant that I now had the entire GK family to care for and we would have to journey without him, truly and forever on our own.

CHAPTER TWO
Baker's Son

I was born the sixth of eleven children on the first day of May 1960, to Mavis and Ephraim Hawthorne. I arrived at about midnight, delivered in bed, at home, in a little hamlet called Border. Located above Lawrence Tavern in the rural St. Andrew hills of central eastern Jamaica, it's a mere dot on the island map, only about half an hour's drive from the nerve center of Kingston, the capital city.

Because of the hilly terrain in Border and scarcity of public transportation, however, Kingston may as well have been a thousand miles away. With no village doctor to summon, and no medical facility nearby, my brothers and sisters had traveled late at night on foot to fetch the community midwife, Nurse Brown, so she could come quickly and tend to my mother. I was told that my delivery was easy; thank God there were no complications, because there would have been nowhere else to turn at that time of night.

Border, like the typical rural Jamaican community at the dawn of the 1960s, had none of the facilities and services enjoyed in the capital city. We certainly had neither mayor nor town hall; nor was there a police station or a health clinic. There was no public works department. Community-spirited citizens like my mom, dad, and other members of the family sometimes provided these amenities, particularly in emergencies. The marvel is that so many residents in Border found creative ways to provide their version of these critical services for themselves. How ironic that without so many urban basics, we were able to have such a big, happy family and thriving business. I remember being fully aware of how nice it would be to have certain public utilities, but was perfectly happy to work around the privations. I guess you could say I grew up with the sensibilities of someone with his gaze on the big city and his roots in the bush.

Sometimes, flooding and landslides caused by heavy rain would block the main road into Border. When it was really bad, we would be cut off for several hours or days until the way could be cleared. The situation reminded us of how strange it was that an island with so much rain and so many rivers could have so much trouble supplying everyone with water.

The exact geographical location of Border often came up as an issue for debate. While we considered ourselves St. Andrew people, our house was technically in the adjoining parish of St. Mary, as the actual boundary of St. Andrew was marked by a little shop about one hundred yards below our house. The technicality only arose in conversation on those occasions when people asked us what was so special about Border or how a place that seemed neither here nor there got its name. Not big enough to be a town, Border developed in the same way many other little hamlets did all over Jamaica at the end of slavery and the so-called Apprenticeship period that followed. Once the free-labor era ended in 1838, African-Jamaicans abandoned plantation life in droves, and many sought slightly more respectable work with merchants and shippers in the port towns. Others literally headed for the hills.

My ancestors chose the mountains to create their idea of a New World. It isn't clear what all the various motivations were for choosing to live where there were no roads, no access by cart or buggy, no running water, and no significant impact by the central government. It does seem likely, though, that those folks were in search of self-determination, closeness to God, and physical inaccessibility by those who may have considered reinstating a forced-labor economy.

The British colonial government of the day allotted some freehold property to the former slaves, but abolitionist Baptist ministers acquired most of Jamaica's ex-slave property for them, establishing free villages like Sligoville in the St. Catherine hills. The tracts they carved out were far away from the flat land on which the plantocracy made its fortune, where news was made, where the fine ladies held tea parties, where the fancy carriages of leisure and the working carts of industry ran around in pursuit of influence and prosperity.

Their successes marked the beginning of an independent peasantry in Jamaica where free farming communities made an honest living, praised their God, and raised their families. The names taken by these communities in my corner of the world tell their own post-slavery story of freedom, optimism, and enterprise: Freedom, Freetown, Unity, and Mount Industry, to name a few. While many of these "free villages" had some fertile (if shallow) soil, where crops could be profitably grown for sale as well as for subsistence, many were often dangerously unstable and prone to erosion. Border was one such place.

Like many other Jamaicans, I return to my hometown as often as I can. For us, the original home is not just some abstract place of ancestry that lives only within the context of a special ethnic festival or nostalgia inspired by a traditional recipe that lingers in notions of our heritage. For

Jamaicans, home is more than a physical location. Those of us who have emigrated, therefore, always genuinely have two homes.

In March 2007, my old high school, Oberlin, was celebrating its sixtieth anniversary. I made a special trip back home to join the festivities. I had made several pilgrimages to the school in the past, bearing gifts for the administration as well as deserving students, and a year earlier I'd been there for a memorial service honoring my father. This time it was different; it was my first trip to Jamaica since his passing. It was also special because my former teacher, Ms. Thelma James, was now the principal of Oberlin. Of all my teachers, she was the one who had exerted the greatest influence on me. She was a disciplinarian who always reminded me that she expected great things in my future. I can only hope that in some way I've lived up to her expectations.

I listened to Ms. James call me "our own boy from west rural St. Andrew." She said she remembered my self-reliance, respect, and strong work ethic. For my part, I remember her spanking me fairly often, but I bear her no ill-will. Ms. James was still a powerfully built woman and commanded that peculiar type of respect that only a Jamaican senior schoolteacher can. To illustrate this, the morning's crowd of Oberliners magically parted and rippled as she approached, and though they had been chattering and fidgeting while announcements were being read at morning assembly, everything changed when Ms. James took the podium.

"Seventh grade girls . . . !" she called out to an entire group that was not yet dead quiet. That was all the children needed to hear. Things calmed right down throughout the hall.

On our way onto the school grounds, I remembered we had seen some students waiting outside the gate; the guard had kept them out on Ms. James's instructions. There was some precedent for this action; she had made the national news some months earlier when she locked out hundreds of students who had arrived late for morning assembly.

"I'm a proud graduate of Oberlin High," I told the students in the auditorium that day, "and all the discipline I learned in life I got right here." I also recalled my old principal the Reverend Richmond Nelson and his powerful inspiration while I was a student there. Once, he told me that I'd soon be ready for the world just like the upper-school students who were about to graduate.

"Who, me?" I protested. "But I'm just a seventh grader!" I imagine I was already ambitious in some way, but I think Reverend Nelson was probably the one who lit that first fire, making me feel I should purposefully plan for my future. He made me feel like I'd be a man soon enough, one who would need a home and a car and things for his wife and children. From then on, I agreed that it wasn't too early.

One important outcome of this special visit was my decision to deepen my relationship with the school. To that end, though Golden Krust had given frequent assistance to Oberlin before, I instituted a program which provided annual cash awards for the top students, as well as incentives for several other students who maintained an A average throughout the academic year. I look forward to the annual presentations and the enthusiasm the students show for their peers' academic achievements.

The last time Golden Krust had given cash prizes to Oberlin students, my accounts department reported that several months had gone by without any of the checks being cashed. I was baffled, wondering if the students felt that the money they would get from the bank was not worth their effort. Only later did I discover that the youngsters had neither the bank accounts in which to make the deposits nor the identification cards with which to cash the checks.

This time, I made sure that representatives from a prominent bank were on hand to welcome the students into the world of thrift by establishing accounts on the spot for each one of them. The youngsters' parents were also brought in to ensure identification.

Amazingly, the adults had no IDs either. What happened next had a profound impact on me. It reminded me of how many innocent ones are derailed in life before they get started—if they don't have the right structure and support. As the children went up one by one, the bankers, resorting to creativity and the wonders of genetics, let the kids use their resemblance to their parents as sufficient proof of identity!

After the festivities at Oberlin, I drove up to the Norman Hawthorne Basic School, which is named for my grandfather, founder of our home church, the Bible Truth Church of God. Grandpa also served the church community as district overseer.

There are so many Hawthornes from that part of the countryside that I amused myself by greeting the students this way: "Who here is a Hawthorne?" Only silence came back. You see, Jamaican children at this age are extremely shy, so I didn't get my answer until a teacher pointed out two children in the group, a serious-faced little boy with a razor-sharp hairline, and a tiny girl who started crying almost immediately. Two Hawthornes.

The school, for children aged three to six, is a tidy but

crumbling little building annexed to the church and sharing some of the flattest land around.

To step through the door was to walk into a rural Jamaican kindergarten of fifty or more years before: one room, too many students, earnest teachers, teaching aids on the walls that just make do, a dirt floor or a surface not much better. In fact, the teachers were quick to point out that the Ministry of Education would close the school if I didn't help with some necessary amenities like the ceiling, the floor, the walls, and much more. My wife and I had only brought book bags, books, toys, and some other educational material for the children. We were merely scratching the surface.

Once we saw the condition of the school and what was needed to make it more modern and habitable, we promised to do more. Soon after, we were able to supplement the salaries of the teachers, repair the school's roof and other parts of the building, as well as donate a television set, computers, a refrigerator, and additional equipment.

That same beautiful afternoon, we took the challenging road up to Paisley All-Age, at the flat top of another hill. I'd gone to school here too, and even taught the ninth grade there for two years after I left Oberlin. I fit the role so well that for a good while, my friends' nickname for me was Teacher Man.

Traversing the rocky hillside of Paisley was in itself a daunting task, fit only for the brave of heart. As a boy it had been easy to run up and down without giving it a second thought. Today I was attempting to drive the rugged path. Like so many other obstacles I had overcome, I was confident I could master the 150-degree right turn to get over the steep slope. My wife Lorna disagreed, screaming her fears from the backseat; and she had every reason to:

the precipice below was over fifty feet deep. Like a warrior facing his most dangerous enemy, I flirted with the edges, turning in small increments, nudging back and forth, gravels flying about wildly . . . Finally, we mounted the last few yards of the hillside . . . and were at last able to breathe . . .

Like so much of rural Jamaica, the place hadn't changed much, except that a car could now drive all the way to the top. We found the old school standing stoutly where I'd left it. I hadn't been a teacher for very long, but memories of the place came rushing back as we headed up the steps and moved through the hallway of the small building.

One grade room I remembered was now the library. The classroom I'd taught in was intact, and we got there just in time to see someone setting up a cotton sheet for a movie screen by pinning it to the blackboard. A laptop computer was ready for the DVD; the new projector was set up and waiting. Preparation was in high gear for a "movie night" fundraiser.

As I lingered there, not a student in view, I began to picture faces, even a name or two. I could almost hear the way the children spoke and played, the things they did well and the stuff for which they needed the most help. Some teachers from my time were still there; I wondered how well I had measured up in their eyes.

The desks, I observed, were the same I myself had used decades earlier. Later on, the students I taught there used them in turn. Now, there they were, with layers of names, past and present, carved and stained into the wood!

We finished with the school visits and finally headed for the Hawthorne homestead, where Papa and Mama had ruled, where the original bakery still stood just next door, where they raised eleven of us—more than eleven, if you count all those Morrisons, grandchildren, and the other citizens of Border who were always in the house. And just like the old days, there was a big meal ready for whoever was coming to visit.

The aroma from the kitchen and dining room took me back twenty-five years into my history the second I crossed through the door frame. Mama had been gone for a while, but the smell of escoveitched fish, ackee, boiled bananas, callaloo, and bread-fruit did much to help preserve her spirit at that moment.

Anyone who has not smelled or tasted traditional Jamaican food is missing a range of beautifully soothing notes like thyme, scallion, coconut oil, nutmeg, and warm-buttered hard dough bread. As usual, it was a lot of food, which I remember could cause frenzied activity at our busy dining table, with all my siblings' overlapping hands and voices competing as we partook of the meal.

For my family, food was a great symbol of Christian kindness. Our parents thought nothing of giving fresh bread and butter to neighbors. Dinnertime was special for them and they followed the adage, *Always cook for passersby— never just for yourself.* Additionally, we came from a community where nobody had a refrigerator, and so everyone depended on one weekly cow slaughter by the local butcher for their supply of beef.

My parents and neighbors would gather at the butcher's to claim a prized piece of the animal. There was often enough to share with neighbors; we would make the sumptuous, traditional beef soup on Fridays, and even have some parts of the cow set aside, preserved in salt for use during the following week. I remember also that my mother had a technique for cooking beef that preserved its integrity for days on end.

Mama was at the center of all the household activity,

especially in the kitchen. She was also a great dressmaker and created all kinds of garments for members of the family.

Typically hands-on, Mama also delegated chores to the older siblings. She was Papa's anchor, a devoted mother, prayer warrior and passionate missionary in the church where my father was overseer. With time, as the older children matured, they too became part of a more complex management structure and were given the responsibility of exercising guidance and authority over the younger ones. The older siblings did a lot of the cooking and laundered school uniforms. It was Mama who woke and fed everyone and left the older children to ensure that the young ones were dressed and ready for church. This elaborate division of labor within families is not uniquely Jamaican. Many in Africa and the deep rural American South also have the tradition of investing sweeping parental responsibilities in the eldest siblings.

In addition to their supervisory roles, the older siblings were assigned the chore of fetching water for both the bakery and laundry. Washing clothes by hand was no ordinary task, because it also included ironing khakis for six boys, as well as several cotton uniforms for the girls. After washing, starch made through an intricate manual process was applied to the uniforms to get the pants seams and tunic pleats sharp and straight. Then there was the housecleaning. All the floors had to be kept dark and shiny with handmade wax polish, which was always applied in the traditional way by crawling around on one's hands and knees and buffing the surface with a coconut brush.

It wasn't all fun and games for us younger ones. We also had our own special duties to perform in the running of the bakery, not to mention the endless errands within the community. At bath time, the more adventurous boys took a quick wash of their bodies in the community spring. My sisters used an outside bath stall built with zinc-sheeted walls. They must have had some of the world's quickest baths, because they were always glancing about to see if the way was clear, guarding against any Peeping Toms who might have been lurking nearby.

To the onlooker, it could have appeared that Mama was permanently with child, as several of us were born close together. The explanation was both simple and romantic. Papa was sometimes away for months at a time doing farm work in the United States. Being gone for that long was hard on him and the family, but Papa's resolve to forge ahead and do the best for the family propelled him. He remained a baker, grocery shop operator, pastor, and justice of the peace, but when he had to supplement the family income, he was also a migrant farmer, traveling north frequently for apple and cane harvesting.

Whenever Papa returned, the reunion was so celebrated that the conception of a new Hawthorne was often the result. One day my sister Novelet, quite innocently, but with that hint of reproach that grown daughters sometimes throw at their mothers, asked, "Mama, why you always having so many babies?" Mama was livid, and Novelet felt her hand that day. Not even the eldest of us was immune to physical sanction whenever we got out of line. Nobody else ever again asked why there were so many of us.

The house at Border was actually somewhat bigger than before. This is ironic because hardly anyone lives there now (we could have used the extra room when we all had to sleep two and three to a bed). Nowadays when I visit, I always notice how small the room space seems, even with fewer people in the house. There is so much life in a home when there are young adults, adolescents, and little kids all mixed into our eleven. All those personalities—reserved, rambunctious, business-minded, authoritarian, academically inclined—combined to make the family vibrant, dynamic, and larger-than-life.

The little reunion was tinged with some sadness too, when I thought that Ms. Pat, this gentle woman who had prepared the day's meal, and who married and moved in with Papa after Mama died, would be our last close generational link to him.

Though we'd been at the house for hours, and I had even found time to stroll through the old adjoining Hawthorne & Sons facility and look up at the sky through where its roof used to be, it seemed as if we were there for mere minutes. Hurricane winds had stripped the bakery annex, but there was enough of the work tables and machinery parts left behind to speed me back to when we spent so much time there, working and learning.

The trip back to Kingston may as well have been a dream. No sooner had we turned the car around than I saw a figure heading down the slope on foot. He wore rags and was dusty from a day spent walking up and down the road. I instantly knew who he was, because he always seems to be nearby when I visited. He often waits around for any of the Hawthorne boys to show up, and I feel certain that his mind is in a time warp in which dirty and clean are relative, where there's no point getting yourself together if it just means falling apart again.

"Hey PeWe!" I shouted to the hulking figure, slowing the car down to a crawl beside him. "Not gonna wash off today?" I asked. His back was still turned to us.

"Plenty time fi dat," he said without turning around.

"You know who's talking to you?" I asked. He stopped walking altogether, and with his head still averted he answered, "Yeah man—Milton."

"No, man," I shot back. It was as if he preferred somehow to focus on something in his mind's eye, not the reality of my voice or my face.

"Oh!" he said, alert and full of focused recognition now. "Is LoLo . . . !"

He finally turned fully to face me. PeWe was certainly from our age group, but he looked twenty years older, no doubt because of general overexposure—and whatever had caused the knot in his mind.

"Yes—it's LoLo," I chuckled back, remembering a dozen true adventure stories from my youth in which that was my character's name. I talked with him for a while, reminiscing about the old days and updating him on how things were with my family. As I put the car in drive and slowly pulled away, I knew he would keep seeking his seemingly attainable objective, only to fail and come back down again.

Ten yards down the road, totally unexpectedly, was a smallish man headed in the opposite direction, up toward the house. Just by the awkward way he hung his left arm by his side, gesturing and hailing me with his right, I knew who he was. Alfred Anderson—Maas Feddie. Now there's a grim reminder of old bakery technology, I thought to myself.

It all came back to me. Alfred was one of Papa Hawthorne's original baker's hands, a man of experience with bread making in an era when trade skills like masonry, carpentry, and welding defined a significant number of Jamaican men. The bakery had a kind of virile, talkative type on staff, and there was always a story being told or somebody mouthing off to someone else. Sometimes things got heated. In fact, Alfred got his other nickname, Dus-Out, because he'd literally been "dusted out" one day, punched down by one of his peers during an altercation at work. It's unclear what exactly happened on that other unfortunate day, the one that changed his life forever, but they say Alfred was cleaning the dough breaker while it was still running. He'd done it before, but this time he was distracted by the usual atmosphere in the bakery, and got his hand caught in the machine. Maas Feddie lost much of his left hand that day. I stopped and asked how things were with him. We chatted awhile before I continued down the road.

Soon, we had left Border's limits and were headed toward Lawrence Tavern. I fully expected to know everyone walking along the road. There weren't many pedestrians that day, but sure enough, I spotted the unmistakable figure of a Rastaman pushing a bicycle up the steep hill toward us. He wore all denim, festooned with patches of Ethiopian flags; around his neck, there were brightly colored ribbons and too many chains and pendants to count.

As we got closer, I recognized the vacant look in the familiar eyes. It was my boyhood partner in agriculture, Clifton "Peeler" Morrison. Peeler had been the one who helped me tend my stock of chickens, pigs, rabbits, and guinea pigs—the first business I ran as a child. I told him I'd been up at the house, and we talked about nothing in particular for about ninety seconds. Though we had some regular-sounding banter, I knew Peeler was no longer playing with a full deck. Our short conversation was one of the same old ones, a repertoire he preserved and performed artfully. After I finished sharing my latest news with him, Peeler bade us farewell and headed up the mountain. I know that he'll keep on making those pointless bicycle trips down to Kingston and back. I also know why he's like that.

"Stay away from that Manchester weed!" I shouted in his direction as I drove away.

There must have been a point in time where all four of us—PeWe, Maas Feddie, Peeler, and LoLo—were essentially the same kind of youngster, imagining what wonders lay outside of Border, operating some kind of microbusiness, or just generally trying to make sense of things.

It dawned on me then, as we descended the hills back to Kingston, that with a few different twists in the road, I could have been any of these other three men, disfigured by injury, displaced by the influx of imported meat and bread—or maddened by ganja smoke forced into an incompatible constitution. I couldn't help recalling stories like the mythical trip to St. Ives or quests from the Greek fables. The out-of-body feeling I had meant that I was now the storybook character who meets a series of significant personages, then tries to decode the signs along the way. There was no way to know what meanings to take away from the encounters, but I couldn't help feeling that there were many people who have had an enormous impact on my life, often without their even knowing it. I recognize that in some ways, these three have influenced me in a big way.

CHAPTER THREE
Family Foundations

Along my life's journey, I've received more abundant blessings than I could have imagined—and certainly more good fortune than bad. I've also had mentors, particularly at church and school, who gave me priceless guidance and encouragement. Nothing prepared me, however, for the sterner challenges of life; gave me an orientation to business; taught me the value of cooperation and bolstered my confidence the way growing up in a supportive, Christian home did. There was so much love and warmth within my immediate and extended family that I always felt that no matter what we lacked materially, we were pretty well off compared to anyone else in the community.

The undisputed head of the family was Papa, who I also called Pops, and who was known within the community as Uncle D or Maas Buddus. His leadership and moral authority extended beyond our family into the entire community. He was an uncommonly kind man whose selflessness went way beyond the mere public-relations gestures of a community businessman. He often satisfied the needs of strangers ahead of his own family's wants, to the point where he was distressed after returning home from his regular sojourns in the United States with gifts for friends, only to hear one ask, "So dis is all you bring back from 'Merica?" Such was his sincerity that he remained undeterred by the comments of those who weren't satisfied with what he brought back for them. That respect and admiration he enjoyed was a source of pride for all of us.

Mama, on the other hand, was the disciplinarian, with special emphasis on the commandment about honoring mother and father. Looking at that angelic face, anyone might think she was reluctant to punish us, but my mother could spank with the best of them. She also made sure that there was enough to eat, that older siblings were managing the younger ones, and that Papa had the support he needed for his roles in the bakery, church, and the community in general.

We all went to church every weekend, regardless of weather or anything else. There was Sunday school in addition to midday services where my father officiated. In order for the Hawthornes to make an appearance, the large family had to get ready in shifts. Once Mama was ready to leave, off she went, and it was the responsibility of the older ones to awaken, bathe, dress, and very often physically carry the little ones up the hill to church. For those who never grew up with that experience, the routine of school, work, and church could seem awfully regimented. But as far as I was concerned, there was fun to be had in every aspect of these rituals. For me, there was no situation that a ready smile couldn't make easier.

The original Hawthorne's Bakery was established in Border in 1949, a year after my mother and father got married. Ephraim Hawthorne was so sure he was destined to be a baker that he was making loaves in secret despite being strongly encouraged by his father, Norman, to become a tailor, a vocation that was then a more profitable and respectable trade. But my dad was determined to bake bread, practicing the craft every chance he got.

After moving from their original home in Paisley, my

father's home district, my parents settled in Border and set about establishing their own baking enterprise, Hawthorne's Bakery. My parents must have been so full of energy and optimism in those days as they started a family and worked hard to make a go of the new business.

It wasn't long before the distinctively sweet smell of his hot bread and the sound of bakery equipment became a fixture with the citizens of Border. By the time the bakery changed its name to Hawthorne & Sons, the place and its bread were central to village life.

The business was not just a unique novelty in Border, however. It was also a source of pride for the community. The bakery seemed to be all that the citizens of Border had for comparing their community with the neighboring "metropolis" of Lawrence Tavern.

Bread was our primary product in those early days, but other standard baked treats like buns and bullas joined the list as well. Family life after that became centered on the bakery, and we siblings were to learn very early that getting the product right and marketing it successfully required cooperation, reliability, and going the extra mile. This perhaps explains why we are all so protective of each other and have always pushed ourselves to succeed.

Within the Hawthorne household, both the residence and the bakery came alive just before dawn. Since there was neither tap water nor electricity for nearly all of the twenty-one years that I lived in Border, there was always a lot to do in the mornings to get the family and bakery up and running. Of course, everyone in the large and constantly growing family had a personal ritual for waking up. Those who didn't have an internal clock set for four a.m. were awakened by the noise of water drums, machinery, and voices starting up a whole catalog of industrial functions.

"Leggo mi foot!" Papa would yell as he walked through the house and into the adjoining bakery. It was his ritual, his way of reminding us that he was in charge and that it was time to get cracking. "Letting go of his foot" simply meant not holding up progress. Then, a familiar series of commands followed: get ready for school, get to work, and let's start baking some bread.

That early in the morning, everything was cold. The floor, the water down at the spring, and the misty air that hung heavily over Border's mountainside all carried a serious chill. I was not one of those children brave enough to jump into the frigid water, but I usually got my comeuppance anyway whenever it splashed down my back as I carried it home on my head.

Although we went to school religiously and on time, we all had delivery duties before school, during lunchtime, and after the sound of the last bell. As usual, big white flour bags filled with freshly baked loaves would be waiting for the older siblings, who would deliver them to the neighborhood shops. Younger ones were not yet ready for bread delivery. Those who had duties at home had jobs in the business as well, with some of the other children experienced enough to actually help run the bakery. As young as some of us were, we all had an understanding of baking ingredients, correct process, and a good end product, with enough skill attained by teaching and observation to hold our own with the men who worked there. My older sister Novelet, for example, began making the entries in the company books from as early as age twelve.

In the 1960s, Hawthorne bread left the bakery while it was still hot, and was taken entirely on foot, directly to all the homes and tiny shops in the area. Lauris, Novelet, and Lloyd—the three eldest—remember carrying the loaves on their heads into neighboring districts like Mount Charles. For balance, they used the *cotta*, a ropy coil of cloth that helped keep up to fifty pounds of cargo steadily aloft. Those in the district who didn't see them coming could always rely on the shouting from those who proclaimed our approach on foot: "Hawthorne's bread van! Hawthorne's bread van!!"

Some of us have mixed feelings about having heard those words that were so often part advertisement, part taunt. To this day, Lauris isn't amused when she remembers the mischievous voices. Novelet just chuckles at the memory. I guess it just depends on how intensely one felt about it at the time.

Before the advent of sliced packaged bread in the late 1960s, Jamaicans exclusively baked or bought hard dough ("hardo") bread, which had a thick golden crust on the outside and chewy dough on the inside. Usually, it was baked in the traditional large loaf, which was cut into slices much larger than those you get from today's typical supermarket bread. Sometimes, it was produced as a wide, flat shape with a tail and called "duck bread." As a staple of the local diet, "hardo" is served with butter or eggs at breakfast, with meat at lunch, or on the side at dinner. At a beach party or church picnic, it was a must-have with fried chicken, fish, or jerk pork. With a spread of thick jam, bread became a sweet treat and there was hardly a food of any kind to which a slice wasn't a welcome addition.

But baking bread by hand in a tiny rural town is not the best way to make a fortune, and so my family, with all its children and its ever-present payroll, had to be very creative about managing certain business practices, given the limitations. The Hawthorne answer was the use of family labor, not in an exploitative way, but by assigning each member of our large family the kind of task that s/he could perform to ensure the operation of a successful business.

Some of us didn't see our assignments in the bakery as work, because the tasks broke up the more rigid routines of school, family prayers, church services, and Sunday school. For those on the outside, it may have seemed as if the bakery defined our existence; for us, we knew that it was the spiritual and educational development of the family unit that took pride of place. No task in the bakery, no matter how important, was ever allowed to get in the way of school or church. Not with Mama and Papa in charge.

The quality of one's best friends, they say, defines the road on which you walk to adulthood. My best friend, for as long as I can remember, was "Garvey," one of the amazing personalities from Border. His real name is Burnett Morrison, of a family that was often indistinguishable from the Hawthornes.

Both families were large and the Morrison children were always at our house. With so many cousins of the same age, my regular play pals and closest friends were either siblings or cousins. Garvey and I were in the same class for the whole time I attended school in Jamaica. In our early days at elementary school, he went by his given name, Burnett, but once he played Marcus Garvey in the Heroes' Day school pageant at Oberlin High, everyone started calling him Garvey. He and I were two musketeers, and we did everything together. We both loved sports. He was the cricket fan while I grew up loving table tennis. He was there when I dominated the other children at marbles and tic-tac-toe; he helped me launch my business career when at only ten years old, I began rearing guinea pigs and rabbits.

This is where it all really started for me, with my father advising and encouraging me, often saying, "So you want to run it on your own . . ." Papa would give me stale bread to feed the animals; I'd find hours after school to feed, water, and watch them multiply before my eyes. Soon, I raised the money to buy chickens, pigs, and goats, and created my own genetic records and profit-and-loss statements. I recorded birth weights and growth rates in order to determine the best yields. Determined to succeed, I devised appropriate market prices every month using cost, demand, and any other factors that helped me keep the venture growing.

Diversified and risk-ready, I raised baby chicks on the upper level of the chicken house. My mother tended the adult birds below. Eventually, I started selling chickens to Mama, who in turn sold them in the family grocery shop. I was extremely proud of the fact that I had begun to create wealth.

From my perspective, the achievements of my parents seemed superhuman. My dad always seemed to be able to afford to purchase the baking material, acquire more machinery, service the equipment, and pay wages; my mother always found a way to make feeding twenty-odd people a day seem easy. Those were the examples that started me thinking in multiples and seeing the possibilities of seeds becoming forests and eggs turning into flocks.

In time, I would make long trips deep into St. Mary and Portland to deliver bread, with Garvey always there beside me. We had so much fun, it never felt like work. I loved driving, and continued to make the runs long after I became a successful young businessman who could afford to hire drivers. Garvey loved speeding through the countryside, especially so he could lurch from left to right in the sideman's seat, exaggerating the effect of the deep corners.

Sometimes we'd race other vehicles from Annotto Bay to Buff Bay, then wait to race someone from there to Kingston. Surprisingly, we had very little trouble from the police in those days.

In my parents' eyes, Garvey was also something of a bodyguard. Regardless of the neighborhoods that we had to traverse to make deliveries, once Garvey was with me, everything was okay with them. In fact, by the time I was making regular deliveries further east, we became the one bread delivery van that seemed to have the "keys" to the country parts. Going into political strongholds or gunmen's haunts made no difference to us, even though we neither had political party nor gang affiliation.

And so, the Hawthorne & Sons deliveries always made it through. There was the occasional squabble between myself and other teens as we went about our business, but Garvey was always there to intervene and diffuse the situation. He was the one who carried the company line in terms of what my parents expected. Not surprisingly, he was hired by Papa right out of high school to manage the bakery. He stayed there for thirteen years.

Looking back over this period of my life, I now see more clearly the extent to which family unity and support gave me motivation and confidence, encouraging me to step out into the world of business, preparing me for the challenges that I would face as an entrepreneur.

CHAPTER FOUR
Kid Tycoon

As a little boy, I must have seemed like quite the dreamer to many who knew me. I think it may have been a combination of distractedness and internal focus that made me appear to daydream. This also explains why I was an average student who seemed to have his eye more on some faraway prize than on the activities in the classroom.

People said they saw it in me from the beginning, and though nobody could foresee the phenomenal growth of the Golden Krust brand or millions of product units being sold, they say they could tell—whether it was in my acquisition of marbles from the children at school or my management of livestock for profit—that I was headed for something significant. Personally, I feel as if I had a very active imagination, the ability to visualize something and just will it or work it into being. But as I would discover, not every dream leads to a desirable reality, so I always say, when one dream gets dashed, find yourself a new one.

My main dream at that time was to be a minibus driver. I am at my calmest and most clear-headed while driving an automobile. Until I decided to write a business memoir, I never thought of motoring as a metaphor for entrepreneurship and progress, but the more I think of it, the more it makes sense. Of course, there are others who feel as I do, who get behind the wheel in their teens and discover the liberating rush of piloting themselves down the road.

When I first caught the auto bug, however, it was no symbol or clue of my future. I genuinely wanted to drive for a living.

In my case, admittedly, driving was an obsession from an early age. I think it was so for some of my brothers too. And now that it has been so long since these events occurred, I can share them without fear of latent interest from law enforcement officers. I'll begin with my older brother, Leroy. When I was a young boy, I thought of him as the most adventurous guy I knew—tall, dashing, and fiercely competitive. Leroy always wanted to be the best at everything—at sports, with the girls, everything. Not surprisingly, once Papa acquired a delivery van, we were excited to log time behind the wheel for any errand, near or far. And so, the legend of the speedy Hawthorne boys was born.

The stories that still persist have a grain of truth but are often embellished, including one about the "driverless" Hawthorne bread van going up or down the hill, piloted by someone too young to hold a driver's license and too small to even be seen in the vehicle. Other stories tell of our van completing a full round of deliveries in an impossibly fast time.

Our ability to drive placed us above what was considered the norm for country kids. For both of us, skills at the wheel developed quickly, and in doing our chores responsibly, we gained valuable self-reliance along the way. We were the ones who drove down to the local spring to get water using a hollowed bamboo stalk propped up against a rock on the far side. This setup allowed us to channel the cool, clean water into our buckets and drums.

"Spring" is what everyone called the spot, because it was everyone else's water supply too. When the girls fetched water, they would carry it back up the hill on their heads. Sometimes, green lizards would get brushed off a low-lying branch and into their buckets as they walked by. For us, the number of trips happily increased whenever our six open-top water drums tilted and splashed as we raced up the hill in Papa's Austin pickup. We would often get home with the drums half-full of water, but we never objected to driving back down to fetch more.

For a few years, my brother Raymond had lived in the flat below my parents' grocery store. He's less than two years older than I am, light-skinned, six-two, and one day announced that he had met the love of his life. Soon, he followed the natural progression of my siblings who moved out once they got married. I was very happy and proud that he'd decided to make this move, though I must confess I was happier to take over his space than the fact that he was ready to tie the knot. Since I was next in line by birth, and therefore heir apparent, I took over the apartment. I truly felt like an adult with my own keys, and with no desire to live in the main house under my parents' gaze.

Legally, I was still too young to obtain a driver's permit. Nonetheless, after doing a quick cost-benefit analysis of a transportation business, I decided to slaughter a hundred chickens and some pigs, sell the meat, and quickly raise the cash to buy my own bus. I also paid a traffic examiner to qualify me for my driver's license so I wouldn't have to wait another year or two to take the test and become fully legal.

I fixed my attention on an old and reliable Volkswagen 1600 Beetle van I knew was going to be sold for six thousand dollars. At the time, I was a veteran of innumerable hours behind the wheel, doing errands and regular deliveries for the bakery. I was ready to be a minibus man.

At that age, there was no greater freedom than being able to come and go at will. My investments in livestock and the little minibus, plus what I derived from working in the bakery, made me quite comfortable for a country kid, and I felt triumphantly independent.

Not having rich kids with whom to compare myself, I felt like I was at the top of the heap for my age group. Anyway, I had more disposable income than the typical youngster in my corner of the world. I was the kid who'd had money in a savings club at school since I was ten, and consistently won school savings prizes for having the most equity every year. Being rich or poor, they say, is always relative to where you're standing—and what you see while you're at that spot.

At nineteen, it felt like the world was mine to explore. After getting the results from my grade-eleven exams, I was forced to conclude that having passed only three GCE O-level subjects, entering any of Jamaica's universities or teacher's colleges was next to impossible. With just the University of the West Indies (UWI) and the College of Arts, Science & Technology (CAST, now UTech) to choose from, only top grades and a greater number of passes than mine could gain entrance.

Both campuses are in the Hope/Mona area of the city, and I recall that on numerous occasions when I took students up from Half-Way Tree to the two schools, I would bid them goodbye by extending my right hand with fingers clutching twenty-, fifty-, and hundred-dollar bills. *If I only had the chance to join them, how much of an accomplishment it would be for me . . .* I honestly felt that way.

Though there was definitely a stigma attached to being a "robot" operator (an unregulated minibus driver), I considered myself a man playing an important role on a route that needed the service. My bus plied a route from Border and Lawrence Tavern to Constant Spring Market and on to Half-Way Tree, the center of everything "uptown" in Kingston.

Passengers trusted me to run with some semblance of a schedule, and so they came to rely on my regularity, as well as my courtesy, two rare commodities in the minibus trade in those days.

After emptying the bus at Half-Way Tree, I would sometimes take it on to Three Miles, the roundabout that filtered traffic onto Marcus Garvey Drive and Spanish Town Road, the main industrial corridor to the west of the city. This was always a quick way to pick up a load and some extra money before going back up my mountain. But the practice had its own dangers. The crowd that usually headed west was a little rougher that those I recognized on the regular route from Border and Lawrence Tavern, so I had my cousin Frederick Hawthorne accompany me as often as possible when I was going that way.

Having Frederick along wasn't always the cure-all I expected. He wasn't the biggest kid, but he often made up for it with attitude and lip. We both knew our limits, though. On the Three Miles trips, we were often afraid of the folks who rode the bus, and knew we wouldn't be tough enough if a passenger refused to pay—or worse, rob Frederick of the stack of folded notes he clutched between his fingers.

"Mi can't stand up to dem man ya," Frederick would protest of his "shotgun-riding" role. "If dem hol' you up, jus' give dem everything!" It wasn't unusual to give away the odd free ride. And that wasn't to be the only unorthodox thing I did with my bus.

For a couple years, it was my habit to shut off the VW's engine on my way down Stony Hill Road, just before Red

Gal Ring and Long Lane, where the grade is steep and where I had built up enough momentum to coast for most of the way down. That distinctive Volkswagen whistle in the motor would became a whisper as if the bus had somehow switched over to clean electric power. I wasn't an environmentalist saving the planet; I was trying to get the most from a gallon of gas. Near the end of the hill above Manor Park, I would punch and release the clutch, kicking the 1600 back to life. I had no idea that using brakes instead of compression to slow down with a full load would wear down my brake pads so quickly—or that jumpstarting the hurtling VW in a low gear was murder on the engine.

So the motor died and the biggest investment I'd ever made was about to perish as well. All my care in finding funds for my venture and working out feasibility with fares, number of trips, and fuel consumption was for nothing. How on earth was I going to replace the vehicle?

It took awhile, after making frequent repairs and buying brake pads, to eventually come to my senses. I forgot about trying to buy a new van. Refusing to quit the business, I did some research and grabbed a flight to the Cayman Islands to get a replacement engine. Soon, I was back on the road, never again trying to save fuel by killing the motor on the way down Stony Hill.

For the rest of the time I lived in Jamaica, my VW minibus was my most prized possession. I used it for paying passengers, bread delivery, the occasional excursion to Kingston's Royal Botanical (Hope) Gardens with the neighbors' children, and as auxiliary transportation for members of my father's church.

By 1980, I was flying high. Now more independent as well as mobile, I wanted to spread my social wings a bit more. Until then, I'd only had close friends inside my family, and all of them lived in my neck of the woods. I wanted to meet more people my age, and girls other than the ones I saw around my district.

Others may have joined a sports team or Boys Scout club; I bought some hi-fi equipment and established my own party sound system. I called it Sir Wass (Wasp) International Hi-Power. Our speakers were midsized and the amplifier must have been underpowered, but with the public that I'd built up from being an attentive minivan driver and personable delivery man, it wasn't long before Garvey and I found a base of operations. Just like we did when we drove interparish to deliver bread, we took the seats out of the VW at party time so that the vinyl records, speaker boxes, turntables, and amplifiers would fit.

Glengoffe in nearby St. Catherine provided a center more populated than Border, with a tradition of popular weekend dances. It also had more young women than any other place around. The dancehall form of Jamaican music was just coming into its own, and that added to the wide range of dance, comedy, and roots music styles from which to select. We were in heaven.

I remember once that there was another dance scheduled for Glengoffe on the same night we were to play at one of our regular venues over there. Our competition had the services of Black Scorpio, a "big sound," as that caliber of sound system is known. Sure, our equipment sounded okay, but we were nowhere near their heights. We set up as usual, and the crowds came. Michigan and Smiley's hit "Nice Up the Dance" put it perfectly:

> Dance haffi cork
> Liquor sell off
> Promoter and his idren haffi laugh . . .

We discovered later that the Black Scorpio "session" (dance) was attended mainly by speaker boxes, sound crew, and not much else. Their dance had flopped. Glengoffe was our turf.

Being nineteen was a time in my life when everything seemed to be flowing perfectly. I was healthy and strong, with loyal friends. Everything was going for me: I had a loving, close-knit family and a new bachelor pad in the basement, now that five of my siblings had married and moved away from Border. My sound system was doing well and holding its own against challengers. Somehow, I was able to manage teaching (at my old primary school), running a regular minibus route, taking the seats out on weekends to do my bread deliveries and transporting equipment for Sir Wass on Saturday nights. Of course, after all that, we put the seats back in time to drive folks to Sunday services all around the countryside and as far away as St. Elizabeth in the southwest of the island.

As Jamaican towns go, Glengoffe in rural St. Catherine is known for its jippi-jappa straw craft and agriculture, and doesn't have a large population or any big-city delights. Our particular fondness for this small farming community was a result of one main thing: its high ratio of single girls to boys. For this reason, all of Wass's DJs had girlfriends from the area, so the team had no complaints whenever it was time for a return engagement there.

On one of those weekends when we took Wass out to play in Glengoffe, I met a local girl named Monica, who actually went to school at Oberlin High. Monica was shapely and soft-spoken, an articulate, very bright young lady. Her parents attended one of the local churches in which my father was the chief cornerstone. She filled my eyes and we soon became close friends.

The relationship continued to blossom, and I took every chance I got to visit her. After a whirlwind of dating, my world suddenly came to a standstill when Monica told me she was pregnant. She was my first serious girlfriend; our frequent hangouts were the great tourist attractions and gorgeous beaches which encircled the island. I am sure that at nineteen, one is not ready to be a father, either mentally and financially. This, of course, had me thinking of the enormous responsibility and the fact that I had suddenly grown up. I spent a few quiet days pondering the best time to break the news to my parents and siblings—that I too had joined the ranks of fatherhood, thereby adding to the growing Hawthorne clan.

Fortunately, my family had already gotten wind of the situation. I'll explain . . . It was typical in those days for a young woman to trek to the home of the boy's parents to inform them of her predicament. Typically, drama and recrimination would ensue. Surprisingly, though, my parents were quite calm about the situation. They sat me down and assured me that the child would be cared for, just like all the other Hawthorne nieces and nephews were.

At the time I was leaving home, profound changes were taking place in Jamaican society. Elected in 1972 on a wave of optimism, the administration led by Michael Manley had declared his government Socialist. By 1980, he had lost his popular support. Manley's foreign policy, which included relations with the Soviet Union and Cuba, was perceived as pro-communist, undermining Jamaica's traditionally strong relationship with the United States. In economic circles, Manley's program of nationalization was seen as a deliberate move to marginalize the private sector and perhaps even to annex U.S. assets as Castro had done in Cuba. At the same time, the expansion of free social services for the poor could not be sustained in a rapidly declining economy. The country became increasingly polarized and the flight of brain power, capital, and entrepreneurs reached crisis proportions.

At home in Border, as in other rural communities, the impact of these changes was sharply felt. Some saw these events as a threat to their way of life, while others just sank or swam with the tide.

The election season of 1980 was the most violent in Jamaican history, and a new administration, led by Edward Seaga, was voted in by a landslide. This new government immediately moved to restore the traditional relationship with the United States, and Prime Minister Seaga became the first head of government to be received by the newly elected American president, Ronald Reagan.

Of the new changes in public policy, the one that affected me most directly was the government's decision to privatize public transport. In the period immediately following World War II, public transport service had been provided by a monopoly, the Jamaica Utilities Company; in 1953, the Jamaica Omnibus Service Limited (JOS) assumed that franchise. The government of the day absorbed JOS in 1974, primarily because the "Jolly Joseph," as everyone called it, couldn't survive solely on revenue from subsidized fares.

The privatization process that began in 1980 called for a sharing of the bus routes between the JOS and the Jamaica Mini-Bus Association (JMBA), a consortium of independent bus drivers. Three years later, the JMBA was given the franchise by the Jamaican government to operate the most powerful segment of the public transport system. With privatization came the advent of subfranchised route "packages." It was with such a package that my long-standing ambition to own and drive a Toyota Coaster bus came closer to realization. For a time, I even dreamed of becoming the JMBA president.

This new regime was well-intentioned and brought about serious changes in the way public transportation was provided. Though the plan was meant to create little fleets running tight route packages on schedule, the system quickly became fragmented, mostly due to the entrepreneurial spirit of Jamaicans—and the fact that more than 90 percent of the buses were operated by owners who only had one vehicle. Service was inconsistent. Passenger tickets, though a requirement of the franchise agreement, virtually disappeared from the system altogether.

To top it off, cops and politicians owned many of the little fleets that plied the assigned routes, and so enforcement of the Road Code was often lax. For many motorists and others, this development must have seemed like licensed mayhem. For a man with a van, however, a minibus could be a goldmine on wheels.

Jamaica in the new millennium still sees the minibus driver as something of a heroic figure, and the minibus features perennially in stage productions and songs like "The Blinkin' Bus" by Lloyd Lovindeer and "Mini Bus" by General Trees. In the early 1980s, when many sole operators could own their own bus and business, there was also big demand for illegal buses on underserved routes. Many of the little buses that zipped all over Kingston without the designated red license plates were referred to as "robots" and the practice of running an outlaw bus was called "running robot."

I'm sure that the Toyota Coaster, with its spacious, comfortable cabin and smooth ride, has become the gold standard throughout the developing world, with its twenty-one seats, superior fuel efficiency, good handling, and great street appeal. It is still the vehicle most desired by the independent bus operator in Jamaica. When I was nearing twenty-one, my confidence as a boy businessman was so high and my desire so great that I decided I was ready to acquire my own twenty-one-seat bus.

For two years I had been engaged in a range of small enterprises. Some were less profitable than others, but all formed an important part of my critical entrepreneurial apprenticeship and taught me some invaluable lessons about running a business. I did not know it then, but within a year I would be one of an increasing number of Jamaicans seeking a brighter future in a new land of opportunity, leaving the Old Country behind. My days as a kid entrepreneur were numbered.

When I left Jamaica in 1981, I wasn't just leaving family, friends, and thriving business interests behind—I was also leaving a pregnant young girl, the gender of whose child I didn't even know. Haywood Hawthorne would arrive in the world on the first day of September in 1981, five months after my arrival in the United States. One of my regrets is that I had to be away in the States and not with them when Haywood was born. Nevertheless, he was well taken care of by his mother, myself, and my parents, despite the fact that I was away.

My son, who made me extremely proud to be called Dad for the first time, spent his early years living with his mother in Jamaica. Being an educator herself, Monica enrolled him in the best elementary school available. For a time, he also lived with my parents in Border. Several summers would see him travel to New York to visit, and before each trip to the city during school breaks, he couldn't wait to join me, my wife Lorna, and his brothers and sister. Finally, in 1996, he emigrated to the States to join us for good.

CHAPTER FIVE
Going to America

For as long as anyone can tell, Jamaicans have emigrated to the United States. Indeed, even before the thirteen British North American colonies claimed their independence as the United States of America in 1776, contact between many of the American colonies and Jamaica had already been well established, largely due to the island's key role in world trade as a top producer of sugar, rum, and other products.

The first Jamaican to establish a major presence in the United States was John Brown Russwurm (1799–1851), who graduated from Bowdoin College in 1826 to become one of the first blacks to graduate from an American college. He is best remembered as the coeditor of *Freedom's Journal*, the first newspaper in the United States to be owned, operated, published, and edited by African-Americans.

It was American investment in the Jamaican banana industry in the second half of the nineteenth century, however, which established the strongest commercial links and emigration between the two countries. Banana boats would bring passengers to the island and then return with cargo to U.S. ports. Later, a big boost to immigration from Jamaica to America came after thousands of Jamaicans were recruited to assist in the United States–led Panama Canal project. Once the canal was finished, many of the Jamaican workers settled permanently in Panama, or left from there for America.

The flow of immigrants from Jamaica to the United States is so strong that just about every Jamaican who is not being "filed for" knows somebody who is. Among the Jamaicans who emigrated to the United States in the first waves was Marcus Garvey, who built the largest Pan-African organization in the world. During the Second World War, many Jamaicans were recruited to work in agriculture and in the nondefense industries.

Over time, hundreds of thousands from the island have emigrated to America. Within one generation, the offspring of Jamaican immigrants established a major presence as professionals, as well as in public administration, business, the armed forces, politics, entertainment, and academia. Some of the outstanding names include the former top American general and later Secretary of State Colin Powell; the distinguished academic professor Orlando Patterson; and the leader of the Black Muslims, Louis Farrakhan. In sports, Jamaican athletes have been coming to the United States on track scholarships since 1943, when Olympic legend Herb McKenley enrolled at Boston University. Jamaicans continue to be among the most sought-after recruits in college athletics, including my niece Trisha Hawthorne, a transplanted Jamaican who has shattered many records at the University of Connecticut and now proudly represents Jamaica.

Some immigrants, like world champion gold medalist Sanya Richards, compete for the United States, while Jamaican Patrick Ewing, who left the island as an adolescent, is considered one of the most outstanding professional basketball players ever. In the field of entertainment, the descendants of Jamaicans are equally prominent. They range from Alicia Keys, Keshia Knight Pulliam, and Grace Jones, to The Notorious B.I.G., and Busta Rhymes. Adventurous

Jamaicans like Kool DJ Herc went to the Bronx and helped create hip-hop using their sound-system wattage and their vocal "toasting" over beats.

Unfortunately, not all make a positive contribution and some have tarnished the good name of Jamaica within the American community. But like many other immigrant groups, Jamaicans are fully integrated into American life and citizenship. Still, even some of the most settled Jamaicans remain preoccupied with the intention to return home—and return home permanently. Although many never actually make that return trip, the desire never gets less intense. Unlike other immigrant groups who typically make "going to America" a one-way journey, Jamaicans see no irony—and therefore have no internal conflict—over the duality: *I am fully American until I go home to Jamaica one day.*

I should have realized that joining my big sister Lauris in America was inevitable. The signs were already there. For example, though I had a U.S. permanent visa before he did, my brother Milton left as soon as he got his papers and joined her in New York City. I was not as eager to get on the plane. This process was going to work like so much else in my family; if something was decided for a sibling born close to me, it would soon be chosen for me as well. We were just never going to all grow up and coexist in the house as adult siblings, the way it works on American television shows like *Dallas.* There were eleven of us, and each in turn, beginning with the eldest, would leave home to determine his/her own future.

I had seen movies and TV shows on our gas-powered television, the one that people in the district would come by to watch, camping out on our front porch and craning their necks for a glimpse of the action. The people on the screen had a lot of everything over there, and it seemed as if things were always exciting, a great life just waiting there for the taking. But life was already great for me in Jamaica and there had been no need to change that. I had just become a man and was coming into my own. I felt like I had already found a paradise, and so the other one in America was irrelevant, something perhaps for another time far in the future.

Then, like a diagnosis of terminal illness, word came that my U.S. permanent residency had been approved. Given a specific time within which I was to travel to the States, not a single cell in my body was ready to go. Everybody knew it too, but there were preparations to be made, the "natural order" of things to be followed. The inevitability of the next in line had caught up with me.

I delayed my departure date in every way I could, but before I knew it, I was giving up my beloved VW minibus to one of my older brothers, Raymond, so he could make a living. My sadness about the bus was tempered only by the fact that I was able to give him such a valuable gift. In some ways, it was all I had in the world. Aston Morrison, one of my cousins (who now works at Golden Krust), got my three pigs, the last remnants of my boyhood empire.

On the eve of my departure, friends and family held a huge send-off party at the house in Border. The event made for a bittersweet time as folks from the church congregation helped to make merry or pray for me in earnest. Others simply wept.

The next day my parents, some siblings and closest friends—nine of us in all, I think—went to the airport to see me off. I put on my best suit, a light-gray gabardine, over a beige shirt buttoned to midchest with the collar folded over my jacket lapels.

Those events are all a blur now, and it took an examination of photographs for me to remember exactly what I wore and who came for the ride to the airport. The pictures show Densford Clarke, Ainsworth Henry, Garvey (by my side as always, and lost in the same sad trance as I was), Frederick Hawthorne (my cousin and minibus sideman), and Raymond, holding Lauris's little daughter, Nataki. The smiles were brave but thin, and all these guys and I who considered ourselves cool and unflappable spent much of the day crying like babies.

Finally, after my pops and mama, stoic as ever, had said their goodbyes, I was turned loose with rubbery legs, bereft of my little kingdom. The boys who had come to see me off went up to the waving gallery so they could pick me out as I crossed the tarmac and climbed the steps up into the plane. I gave them my final goodbye wave. It didn't take long for everything to sink in: I was leaving home and leaving my parents. I was also leaving my bread customers, my passengers, all my friends, all my girlfriends, and with a baby on the way . . .

CHAPTER SIX
No Paradise in the Bronx

I'd been on an airplane before, but only on short trips that ended with my return to Jamaica. Now I was going away for good, to a new country and climate with all its unknowns. After what seemed like an eternity in the air, we finally began the descent from 35,000 feet into John F. Kennedy International Airport. After bouts of hard crying before and during the flight, I was unprepared for the beauty of the approach over Long Island Sound and the lights of the airport and city. The clear night afforded spectacular views of the New York skyline, including the Twin Towers of the World Trade Center. The sights were encouraging and exciting, dulling some of the pain.

After following the disembarking passengers and walking purposefully along the corridors of the airport, I got to the grand entrance of the immigration hall at JFK, carrying my big, all-important document. *This envelope can only be opened by a U.S. immigration officer*, it read.

Upbeat and anxious, I got in line. About forty-five minutes later, after inching along and reading the welcoming posters on the walls and scanning the faces of the passengers coming in from all over the world, I presented my papers. I was processed, then ushered into customs. *This is the kind of place that embraces immigrants*, I kept thinking.

I landed in New York City on the night of May 2, 1981, one day after I turned twenty-one. It was the last day of entry eligibility on my visa. After leaving JFK customs, I was met by Lauris. My brother-in-law Rupert Campbell had brought her to the airport in his nice 1978 Cadillac. In that brief reunion at the airport, I noticed that she had acquired many of the mannerisms and maternal instincts of our mother. It was the last time I would think of her as just my sister Lauris.

When we drove in from the airport, I could feel my eyes becoming increasingly saucerlike as I got my first exposure to the wonders of New York at night. I still recall the fascination of looking out at the well-lit streets as we headed through Queens. The traffic moved easily and although the distance from the airport to our destination seemed far greater than I was used to traveling, we made good time.

We crossed the Whitestone Bridge into the Bronx. The unusual stop at the toll booth had me baffled. I had never seen or heard of an occasion where one pays to cross a bridge. Further, I couldn't understand who the money would go to. Scanning the residential neighborhood along the wide and busy Fordham Road, I noticed that in contrast to Jamaica where people parked their cars inside their gateway, the vehicles were parked on the street. Still, in a city where so many people lived and worked, things looked pretty orderly as far as I could tell. Finally, we arrived at my sister's house in the Bronx. Safe inside the gate, I was so emotionally and physically spent that I found myself only looking forward to some welcome rest.

Once inside the house, however, I felt reenergized by the reunion with my brothers as we all got together in the living room, chatting for hours. My sister, who normally would have been at work, had taken the night off. While I was catching up with the others, she heated up some fantastic pork chops with macaroni and cheese. That delicious dinner was like nothing I ever had before.

I really felt welcome and at home. The conversation kept me upbeat. I was now looking forward to being even more productive and successful in this new, exciting environment. I wouldn't miss the bakery chores and the various restrictions I'd known while growing up. Here was television, electricity, presumably all kinds of food we couldn't get back home—as well as the novelty of water from the tap.

As we all chatted and bonded at Lauris's home, my earlier impression was confirmed. She was no longer just my big sister. Since I last saw her, she had taken on a far more central role in the life of her siblings. For all intents and purposes, she had become the anchor of our family in New York, taking on the responsibility of bringing her family up from Jamaica to make a good life in the States. As a result, everyone looked to her for parental leadership. It is not clear when we all got used to calling her "Mother," but by the time I arrived in New York she was already answering to it. I guess it made sense, as all of us, like her children who lived with her, were definitely under her care. It wasn't that she replaced Mama at all; she just headed the American branch of the Hawthorne family and was in charge, even more than she had been in Jamaica.

When all the pleasantries were over and I was finally ready for bed, I asked, "Where's my room?" Someone promptly escorted me to my brother Charles's room. I soon realized that the space was also Milton's. Then it hit me— like that queasy roller-coaster feeling you sometimes get in the pit of the stomach—that we would be three to a bed again, just like in Border. And by some bizarre coincidence of birth order, it would be the same three boys sleeping together again. Only now we were grown men of eighteen, twenty-one, and twenty-eight.

Sleeping foot-to-head and head-to-foot the way we used to was going to be a problem. I was still hoping that it was some kind of cruel joke, until I saw the other two take up their positions. As the newest arrival, I settled into the remaining space. Although I had arrived in New York, it was like I was bizarrely back home in Jamaica—and during the days before I had my own flat at that! Luckily for me, Milton and Charles had their own ladies and were not home most nights.

On the first morning in the Bronx, I woke up to find the other members of the household already showering or getting dressed. Before I could get my bearings, Milton left for work at Bowling Green Pizza; Charles, the mathematician, was off to classes at LIU and "Mother" went to her home-care day job. By eight o'clock, the house was empty. To make matters worse, there was no breakfast left for me and certainly no sumptuous morning ritual of fresh bread from Hawthorne & Sons Bakery. I suddenly felt thoroughly alone in the new and strange environment, consoled only by the feeling that this was probably no different from what thousands of my countrymen had experienced during their first morning on American soil.

By the beginning of the twentieth century, American and Caribbean blacks had carved out a community for themselves east of Eighth Avenue in Manhattan, between 130th and 145th Streets, popularly called Black Harlem. One of the best-known Jamaican migrants in this early period was the literary genius Claude McKay, who arrived in 1912 and went on to become one of the dominant personalities of the Harlem Renaissance. While Black Harlem became a vibrant, multicultural melting pot, the Bronx remained very much a white, middle-class residential area.

In the 1960s, the social character of the Bronx began changing as high-rise housing projects replaced traditional residential neighborhoods. Crime rates and antisocial behavior increased at the same time that the area became home to an increasing number of immigrants from the Caribbean and Latin America. They had come with meager savings accumulated after years of personal sacrifice often augmented by family contributions. They knew that their success would determine the fate of those left behind, and were prepared to work long hours under the most difficult conditions to realize the American Dream.

By the time I arrived in 1981, a process of redevelopment had begun to halt the downward slide. This was the Bronx that I awakened to on my first morning in the United States. Adventurer and optimist that I am, I went outside for a walk and found a truly rude awakening as I went looking up and down Morris Avenue. From the voices, music, and whatever else I could hear, I discovered that it was predominantly an immigrant neighborhood, mostly Latino. I couldn't believe it was the same place I'd seen the night before. In the light of day, I now saw garbage cans, litter, trash bags, and cars as far as the eye could see—which was all the way to Kingsbridge Armory. I had no idea that a neighborhood street could be so long.

Contrary to my fantasy of the night before, I realized that this was nowhere close to being a nice neighborhood. It was a completely different city from the one I'd imagined from watching all those television shows in Jamaica. Man, I thought I'd know New York! *What have I done? What am I doing here?* I kept questioning myself, over and over again. It was a sobering, even frightening reality.

Thinking clearly again, it occurred to me that I didn't have enough money to invest in any kind of enterprise in

America. The money I did have, which might have seemed more than enough to start a small business in rural Jamaica, would not give me any kind of start here. Slowly, I came to the realization that I would have to forget entrepreneurship and find myself a job.

I returned to the house, went upstairs, and got out my little address book full of phone numbers. Determined to reach any of the friendly family voices from the night before, I got busy dialing. I couldn't wait until they got home, so I could talk over all that had been going through my mind, get angles, find out what was possible and what would keep me out of trouble.

Unable to reach a soul, I suddenly realized that I was hungry. I made breakfast, a couple of fried eggs which I ate with bread made someplace on Kingsbridge Road. That was sacrilege, I thought. Until then, I'd never spent much time considering the other bakeries that made bread. The taste of Hawthorne & Sons was all I'd known, really.

Depressed, I watched the clock and waited for my folks to return home. Fortunately, "Mother" and Milton called after a while. Charles's wife Janice also phoned to check on me in the early afternoon. Then my nieces Desrene, Marcia, and Tanika trickled into the house after three p.m., followed by "Mother" about an hour later.

As the house filled up again with familiar faces, I began to feel the warmth of family return. Everyone wanted to know how I had spent my day and whether I had started making plans. With what seemed like military precision, "Mother" prepared the most delicious-smelling pork chops for dinner, but before I could settle down to eat and converse, she said, "LoLo, your dinner's been cooked. I'll have to get a few hours sleep before going to my second job . . ." She was clearly in her nurturing role, but all business as well.

Like so many other Jamaican immigrants, "Mother" had a second job. Hers was a night shift at Kingsbridge Nursing Home. To this day, she doesn't know who initially sponsored her to come up from Jamaica to do home care; it's still a mystery.

At about seven that evening, Milton got home and marked the occasion of my first day with the biggest bottle of beer I'd ever seen—an Olde English 800, I think it was. As we sat on the stoop and surveyed the other stoops all in a row, I couldn't help wondering, *Is this what life is going to be for me? Is this all there is?*

"Mother's" husband Rupert drove me to apply for my Social Security card. Without it, I would have only been able to work at menial jobs and could have counted on nothing above the minimum wage. So, for the next two weeks while I waited for it to arrive, I remained mostly cloistered inside the house. Instead of watching television or exploring the neighborhood, I spent a lot of my time writing letters to friends back home.

With her talent for stretching a dollar and feeding the five thousand, "Mother" had managed to give me an allowance of twenty dollars a week. In those first weeks, most of this pocket money went to buying postage stamps.

I wrote dozens of letters, pouring out my thoughts and fears about the transition and what a big mistake I'd made. I missed everyone and everything, and constantly wondered how far my enterprises would have reached had I stayed in Jamaica. To ease my depression, I tried to keep up with the news everywhere. My good friend at the Border Postal Agency, Miss Banks, sent me newspapers from Jamaica so I wouldn't feel so homesick. I bought the *Sunday Times* and spent the entire day searching the classifieds for job openings. I certainly saw many I would have liked to apply for, but I didn't have the necessary qualifications. As far as I was concerned, the ideal start for an ambitious adult like me in New York City was an office job, but I couldn't type or file or use a computer. Outside of raising animals, all I knew was driving and baking.

Finally, my Social Security card arrived. But three months later, I still had not landed the office job I wanted. I kept thinking, *Is this so much to ask for in the land of opportunity?* At my wit's end, I called Mama and Pops, crying over the phone, begging them to let me come back home. I felt discouraged, and thought I had just about lost all focus. Additionally, I was also getting physically sick, with mysterious aches, pains, and a general malaise often related to depression. I had even started to thoroughly check the classified ads for messenger jobs, circling some that paid no more than the $3.50 minimum hourly wage.

"Sonny, hang in there," Papa would counsel when I talked to him.

After registering at the New York State Employment Agency, I eventually got a job interview. The effort resulted in my first job, working as an inventory clerk at Abraham & Strauss (A&S) men's store on Fulton Street in Brooklyn. Right away, it was clear that I'd have to buy myself new ties and nicer shirts on store credit because my clothing, true to the fashion of the day in Jamaica, was just too colorful for a New York store clerk. Some of my pants were also hopeless for my new life, and I remember that one pair in particular had three colored stripes on the cuffs and the edge of the pockets! My most stylish shoes from home, which had transparent soles, were equally inappropriate for my job. To complete my transformation, I bought a more sober pair.

* * *

A man's shirt in a department store may seem like a harmless and common enough item—until you have to repackage one that's been opened, tried on, and cast aside by a customer. There are pins to replace after the garment, supported by cardboard, has been perfectly refolded. A plastic collar goes under the cloth collar and over the neck button for even more stability. Pins—sometimes a dozen or more of them—are strategically stuck in to keep the folds in place and force the shirt to stay flat. Finally, the pristine shirt is pushed gently back into the plastic bag, ready for handling anew. Putting them back together was specifically my responsibility, but I just couldn't get it right. In fact, out of frustration I started hiding the offending shirts at the bottom of the shelf, hoping my supervisors would never notice. I was wrong.

My first paycheck was not enough to cover the shirts I'd bought on credit. In addition to that minor tragedy, I was not very good at my job. To be honest, I was terrible. And I was frustrated with the entire concept behind my job. *Why are customers opening these packages and not buying them?* As fast as I could fold them, it seemed there was no shortage of customers to open them again. I became even more frustrated as I noticed the ease with which the manager seemed able to refold and repackage the shirts to look brand new.

After three weeks on the job, without mastering the art of shirt wrangling, my stint at A&S ended. My confidence was so shaken that I decided I had to find a way to stay in the game. Instead of focusing on getting a slightly better job, I decided to improve myself by going back to school. Inititally, I looked into the possibility of enrolling in a college that friends or family members had attended. At the time, my brother Charles was at Long Island University (LIU) pursuing his master's degree in mathematics, so being on that campus would have given me advantages and some amount of comfort knowing he was there. But LIU tuition proved too expensive, so I looked to the more affordable City University of New York (CUNY) system instead.

Because a high school diploma, or at minimum a General Educational Development (GED) credential, was needed to apply at CUNY, I had my high school transcripts sent from Jamaica to the CUNY system to satisfy the requirement. I was accepted at CUNY in the fall of 1981, beginning classes in the spring of 1982.

Like some kind of divine intervention, the State Agency soon called to say the New York Police Department (NYPD) would be doing major restructuring, putting more cops back on street duty and hiring civilians for various roles within the department. I applied for a job as an assistant stock handler, a position that paid $11,000 a year, with full medical and pension benefits, plus four weeks' vacation. I felt that I had aced the interview and showed the temperament and eagerness they needed. The clerk also gave me the feeling that I would get the job. I immediately began to fantasize about making more money than I had ever seen, with a wage package that would make me no longer dependent on "Mother." To top it off, the job would require me to work at the NYPD headquarters downtown. I'd be going to an office in Manhattan—it would work out after all!

My thoughts must have carried me away and diverted my focus from the interview, as I suddenly became aware that Ms. Sterling, a personnel officer from the police department, was repeating a question she had already asked.

"Do you have a green card?"

"No, ma'am," I replied, "it hasn't come yet . . ."

I was sure at that point that the interview would be

terminated. Once again, it seemed that the positive results that should come with sufficient effort were being derailed. Since I'd arrived in America, not even my best efforts seemed capable of guaranteeing modest success. My only consolation was that failure would give me a good excuse to head back to Jamaica so I could resume the life I'd been enjoying there. As I contemplated the inevitability of failure, however, I hearard Ms. Sterling's voice again.

"Once you get it," she said, "then you can return. We can't hire you without it, okay?"

The mailman would show up every day between ten and eleven a.m. Without fail, I checked daily to see if my green card had arrived. I had heard that neither rain, snow, nor storm would stop the mail, so that was quite comforting. Each morning, I would look out the window with trepidation and anxiety to see if that government package had come.

Miraculously, my green card arrived a few days later, making me officially part of the American system. Finally, I could stop pacing the floor at my sister's house and quit feeling that I was doomed to live with the depression and disappointment of not having a job. My luck was beginning to change, though some of my shine had come off. I was still an optimist, but I knew that success would never again seem like an automatic thing.

CHAPTER SEVEN
On the Job

I had put a lot of effort into my job hunting and would have settled for a gig as a messenger or as a delivery van driver, the two things for which I was truly qualified in 1982. I'd waited for a long time to be legally able to work until finally, there was a welcome breakthrough in the most unlikely place. I was actually going to work for the police department! I didn't know it then, but my entire life would turn on this new phase of my American experience.

My earlier frustration at not finding an office job didn't make me completely give up on succeeding in America. In some ways, it made me want to improve myself so that I could move up the ladder of success in the same way people on TV and in the glossy magazines did. It made me realize how easily we buy into the idea promoted in the media that everyone has access to American prosperity. I'm not a critic of all that, for experience has taught me that it is actually having a dream that helps to make dreams become a reality for a great many people.

Growing up in Jamaica, I knew the value of education and was sure that going back to school was the only way to achieve professional status. This is the main road that the immigrant communites in America have traveled, with a lot of phenomenal success over the generations. I had read somewhere that immigrants account for half the scientific research workers in the U.S., and make up roughly the same percentage of PhDs in engineering and computer science. So when I enrolled at Bronx Community College, I fully intended to see it through, as many other immigrants had done. As it happened, the lure of $11,000 a year was just too strong. I put college on hold for a while and went off to work for the cops.

On the hot summer morning of August 17, 1981, I rode the subway, via the number 4 IRT line to the City Hall/Brooklyn Bridge station. Up at street level, I walked to Park Row in downtown Manhattan, en route to One Police Plaza, headquarters of the New York Police Department. Freshly scrubbed and punctual, I don't think I have been as eager for anything before or since. The drab thirteen-floor building didn't promise any glamor or excitement, but I was ready for steady, respectable employment.

The officer in charge of supplies, Sergeant Marty Turetsky, was my first contact when I showed up for work. He was a smallish man, with the look of someone you'd expect to meet at the post office or Department of Motor Vehicles. I noticed something fatherly about him—he didn't have that hard edge that you might expect from one of New York's Finest. "Willie Colon will be your partner," he said, in the midst of giving me instructions. The routine, he outlined, was simple: lift, unpack, carry, and stack. *Easy enough*, I thought.

After getting all my procedural details, I was issued a pair of work gloves and a gray police department shirt, then led to the loading area. There was a forty-foot trailer waiting. Against my better judgment, I heard myself saying, "I'll be right back." Willie must have figured I needed a very long and urgent men's room break, because I was in there for a good half hour. Finally, after washing my face and composing myself, I reemerged wearing a huge smile. I'd been inside bawling the whole time, terrified by the prospect of back-breaking labor that lay ahead on the trailer. The shipment on that first day consisted of whistles, duty jackets, pants, and shirts for the next class of new NYPD officers. From ten a.m. to three p.m., we loaded pants, which were packed a dozen to a box. That was manageable enough. The real challenge came when we got to the police duty jackets, those heavy dark-blue ones that keep patrolmen toasty while on the beat. They came in packages of about sixty pounds each. Lifting them off the trailer was one thing; getting them to their destination on the second floor, two hundred yards down a hallway, through a dingy passageway, then up a service elevator to the police department's equipment storage room, was quite another. At the end of the first day, my body felt it had been given as much as it could take.

Back in the Bronx that night, while it seemed like I had been worked over emotionally, I was happy to be in the system, and I was glad to be doing much better than the messenger or delivery man I might have otherwise become.

The following day, it was time to get used to the next phase of police supply work. Senior stock handler Michael Maxwell showed me how to break down the boxes and arrange them neatly on the shelves. It was tedious and mindless work, but at least it was inside. I loved handling those police shirts. They didn't have to be repackaged over and over again with pins and plastic.

By the time we were through, we had unloaded so much stock that it took the rest of the week to break down the packages and make the appropriate entries in the inventory.

I am always fascinated by the events you recall which on

reflection were significant turning points in your life. One such unforgettable memory took place after my first couple of months on the job. Totally unprepared for the first blast of biting cold which came that winter, I would have packed it in had it not been for Marty Turetsky, who handed me a brown corduroy coat very close to my size and just the right weight for the inside-outside work I was doing. It was almost as if he knew I needed it, because I was approaching the point of losing all the feeling in my body.

That gesture became for me an act of generosity that I will always remember and will never be able to repay. Ironically, he doesn't remember giving me the jacket that probably saved me from pneumonia. On the other hand, I have somehow forgotten the day he says I spent or lost a hundred-dollar bill, having mistaken it for a smaller one. Turetsky is retired now, and is easily one of the most active cops on a pension anyone could hope to meet. He helps with walking tours of New York City, leading visitors around the sights while expounding on the folklore of the city. I owe a lot to his patience and fairness.

I remember vividly the first time I caught a glimpse of the secure room that held every caliber of police firearm. At the time, I'd never even seen a gun up close. In Jamaica, you saw a cop's gun in the holster from afar and you never saw private firearms; I was aware of gun-toting criminals, but I'd never had contact with one of them. My curiosity was aroused. *When will I be able to go into that room?* I thought to myself. On the next delivery day, a box truck and a step van came up to the dock for unloading. This time, the cargo was guns.

Working that shipment was a big deal for me. Just handling the unopened boxes felt magical. I couldn't stop thinking about all this police muscle destined for Police Academy graduates, in my hands.

The pistols were divided into two categories: two-inch snubnosed muzzles and four-inch ones. The task took one to two hours, and there was no way the department would let me mistake this cargo for uniforms and whistles. When I began stocking guns at NYPD, I was accompanied inside and out by senior police officers. Turetsky himself watched us work and checked off quantities as the delivery progressed.

In my private moments, I was not entirely satisfied with my job, but nobody ever had a clue about this. I simply kept doing my duties better and better all the time. The more I did the lifting and carrying, the more I stuck to the task and the more trust I inspired among my bosses. I recorded serial numbers from two hundred pistols at a time, and packed the small gun boxes away by color: Smith & Wessons in the blue boxes, Rugers in the yellow. After only five months on the job, they gave me a key to the gun room. Just a kid of barely twenty-one, I was the only civilian in New York City to have access to an NYPD gun room. The routine had me locked into the twenty-by-thirty strong room at nine a.m. and going out for a bathroom break at ten. My sense of humor had a field day. There I was, locked up and in charge of the firearms to be distributed to New York cops!

I was such a good employee that before long I was made a cashier, managing transactions with all the rookies who came in to be outfitted. I showed my mettle as a good numbers guy too, going virtually error-free with stocks and sales. On one occasion, when my parents were visiting, I introduced them to the sergeant, and even showed them the gun room. I had clearly earned his respect, inspired no doubt by my work ethic.

In time, my performance on the job brought its own

rewards. I was getting my college itch back, and it wasn't long before I told Sarge that I wanted to return to school. I wasn't sure if he'd help me figure a way to attend classes and keep my job, but he was certainly impressed by my ambitions. In fact, it seemed he respected me even more for it.

Enrolling in classes meant that I had to find a way to leave work earlier. So I skipped my lunch hour, by just having a quick bite, and changed my hours to the seven a.m.–three p.m. shift. That way, I was able to leave in time to attend classes at four.

In 1982, I moved into a housing project called Hillside Homes. After the many months spent living with my sister Lauris and her family, I thought the time had come for me to start flying on my own. With steady job in hand and most of my homesickness and depression behind me, my sister Jackie, my brother Milton, and I joined forces and rented a three-bedroom apartment. Although we were not tenants in the pure legal sense, we at least looked the part, having gotten the apartment from Cyril Barnett, a good family friend. The rent was subsidized, so we were actually paying $454 a month, including utilities.

The Hillside community is nestled in the Williamsbridge section of the North Bronx, stretching from Fish Avenue to Eastchester Road, covering two square miles. The five blocks of low-rise brick buildings were conceived some time in the 1930s as an urban oasis of playgrounds, workshops, and a nursery school, primarily for the European immigrants who had been crowded into the Lower East Side. But that was before poor management, suburban flight, and other factors brought vandalism, drugs, and deadly violence to the area.

It couldn't have been an easy adjustment for us, especially since we had lived with "Mother" in a private residence, without the usual pressures of living in a large public housing complex of the era. Whatever the original social blueprint had been, Hillside was no longer the utopia that urban planner Clarence Stein had envisioned fifty years before.

At night, there was loud music on the street. Sirens screamed in frustration as cops patrolled the area, losing the fight against the drug hustlers who hawked crack and powder cocaine. Then there was the frequent gunfire . . .

On one or two mornings, I could clearly see a fresh body on the street, put there by the previous night's gunplay. From time to time, bullets would crash through our windows, but on all those occasions, praise God, we were not at home.

The love of my life, Lorna Roach (who later became my wife), was instrumental in helping me meet the goals of homeownership, with more focus on the safety and future of my new son Omar, who was born when I still lived at Hillside. While I lived in the projects, the role of family assumed an even greater importance as violence and danger pushed me to earn more and get out.

Lorna grew up in the Freetown/Maidstone area of Manchester, a parish in central Jamaica, some distance away from Border where I grew up. Although I had toured Manchester various times to operate my sound system and had taken several church trips there with my parents, our paths had never crossed.

Paulette and Lorna Roach were brought up in an environment where life revolved around family, church, and school. The relationship between the sisters was a close one. Both of them shared a commitment to the pursuit of education and spending quality time with family in conversation or prayer. Church was the big priority, and like so many other children in rural Jamaica, they attended more church services than any other form of social activity. Party going had not been part of their upbringing, and so it turns out there had not been even the remotest chance of Lorna attending any of the dances where my sound system played.

Both girls eventually migrated to New York. I had known Paulette's boyfriend Neville for some time, but unbeknownst to me he was secretly playing matchmaker and was on the lookout for nice guys to whom he could introduce Lorna. As fate would have it, she and I finally met at a party in 1983. My gaze was fixed on her high cheekbones and striking beauty. She was no more than one hundred and twenty-five pounds and spoke softly, but she exuded confidence in every word she spoke.

We struck up a conversation, and from that moment I knew fate had brought us together for a reason. For one thing, I saw kindness in Lorna right away. Our first chat was only a few words, but they were enough to etch her image in my mind. As our friendship grew in coming months, a love blossomed as well. It didn't take me long to decide that she was the one with whom I wanted to spend the rest of my life.

Lorna proved to be an exceptional cook, and often baked great cakes and potato puddings. I will always remember some of the masterpieces she has set out on the family dining table.

Lorna says she saw kindness and compassion in me as well. So taken was Lorna that her enthusiasm wasn't even dampened when she called me at the house only to have

"Mother" say, "He's not here!" and hang up abruptly; she simply took it in stride. Poor Lorna didn't realize that my big sister was not trying to be difficult or overprotective, but simply needed all the rest she could get before going off to her night job as a nurse's aide.

Conveniently for our courtship, Lorna's mom worked at the Sombrero Club, a popular working-class West Indian joint in White Plains. We went there often and enjoyed dancing, particularly when the Sombrero's DJ played our favorite slow tunes.

It was 1983 when Lorna joined me at Hillside, after I'd spent a year in the projects. She worked for the Moravian Church at the time; I was already with the NYPD. After a few months of seeing each other, Lorna became pregnant with my second son, Omar. Although we weren't married, the experience was less traumatic for me than when Haywood was on the way. Now I was over twenty-one and knew a lot more this second time around. I thank God for my wonderful brother Milton and sister Jackie who graciously allowed us to continue living in the apartment as my slice of the Hawthorne family began to expand.

That expansion brought immediate financial difficulties, especially as it related to affording babysitters and other expenses that come with raising children. Most days, we were on edge since we were not tenants of record for the apartment and could be thrown out at any time. Lorna had to look for government assistance to help out with basic necessities like milk, orange juice, and eggs. Every six months, she would have to take the long ride to Brooklyn to show her meager paycheck and get requalified for the Special Supplemental Nutrition Program for Women, Infants, and Children (WIC).

We were both driven by a fear of urban violence, and

the powerful urge to protect our new child from such an environment gave us an even greater impetus to get out of Hillside. If we were going to raise children with the kind of education they deserved, the projects would not be the right place for them.

Lorna continued to work up to her eighth month, and was blessed by having very few complications throughout. We welcomed Omar into the world on November 27, 1984. Naturally, we started to talk even more seriously about the prospect of owning our own home. So Lorna, Jackie, and Milton all enrolled in college or trade school with a singular objective: finding better jobs so we could move out of the unsafe and nonprogressive environment at Hillside.

When Lorna had first become pregnant early in 1984, we were already committed to each other, but hadn't gotten married immediately because we could not yet afford the big wedding we would have preferred. Now we had another good reason to get married—and intensify our efforts to establish our own home.

"Lorna," I said one day in a moment of resolve, "it's time to leave the projects and buy a house."

She agreed. Both of us were committed to saving and took financial matters one day at a time, living within our means. By getting a loan from "Mother" and from Lorna's mother, Hyacinth, and saving money through "susu" (a kind of fixed-savings club among friends who take the entire pool after drawing for turns), we had managed to put together the $10,000 down payment, and were scheduled to leave our old place. Then our plans hit a major snag. We couldn't get a mortgage quickly enough to move into the house we had identified at Mickle Avenue in the Bronx. With a whopping 18.5 percent interest rate in the offing, we were stuck. Finally, we were able to get an 8 percent break on the rate, and the owner, who lived on the upper floor of the house, let us live on the ground floor until our mortgage came through, nine months later. The area we occupied downstairs only had one bedroom, with living, dining, and kitchen areas all together. Omar slept with us in the bedroom area. We knew the space was inadequate, but we held on.

The early Reagan years brought high inflation and high interest rates, and families in our income bracket had difficulty affording a home without state assistance. Salvation finally came when we were fortunate enough to fit into a mortgage program offered by the State of New York Mortgage Agency (SONYMA). Through the sale of tax-exempt bonds, the agency served low- and moderate-income families in New York with competitively priced mortgage programs and mortgage credit certificates for home purchase in the state. All the options offered a competitive interest rate, low down payments, no prepayment penalties, and down payment assistance.

After waiting for such a long time to close, we were overjoyed when word finally came that we could now attend the signing over to finalize the purchase. The documents were all signed, the checks disbursed, and time seemed to slow down as my attorney, Orlando Lenti, asked the seller to hand the keys over to us, sealing the deal once and for all. Thanks be to God, through hard work and perseverance, we officially bought the house we occupied on Mickle Avenue in December of 1985, and moved upstairs. Getting those keys in our hands that day gave us an almost indescribable sense of accomplishment and security, the feeling that we were about to unlock the next chapter in our lives.

On July 13, 1985, a bright sunny Saturday afternoon in

the Bronx, we sealed our devotion to each other in an intimate wedding ceremony attended by our parents, siblings, close relatives, and friends.

I think it's difficult for people who have not had the specific immigrant experience to understand what it means to Jamaicans to own their own homes. Perhaps it was the years of harsh tenantship on the island throughout the post-slavery and pre-Independence periods that has contributed to it, but one thing is certain: Jamaicans are obsessed about homeownership, wherever they happen to be. And since housing stock and homebuyer credit are more abundant on average in America, that obsession is far more intense once a Jamaican makes the trip north. Statistics tell this story better than legend can.

In our case, we had strived and pushed ourselves, and we knew we hadn't bought a palace, but we were proud of our first house and thought it was a really nice place—even if it wasn't the warmest, by Lorna's recollection. Still, it was ours, and gave us a sense of progress toward our own American Dream.

We were walking on air. After only four years in the country, I could check off one major objective in life and follow in the footsteps of cousins and other relatives who were also able to buy homes early. We felt a renewed gratitude toward them, because they had served as mentors in this regard.

Once we had acquired a new bedroom set and updated our kitchen utensils, it felt more and more as if we belonged. Soon after we settled into the new place, the clan expanded again. We were blessed with the birth of Monique, followed by Daren less than two years later. This was now truly the Hawthorne home, a possession so valuable to us that it was destined to become the main collateral needed to get Golden Krust off the ground.

With a monthly mortgage commitment and four kids, I found myself thinking more of owning and operating my own business as a means of truly claiming my piece of the American pie. This dream moved one step closer to reality when I registered for accounting classes. I remember being particularly fascinated by the income tax returns process. I took the courses seriously and it was not long before I felt I was ready to assist fully with individual income tax returns. After all, there was a guaranteed market for that service among the growing number of NYPD staff and police (mostly rookies), who needed help with their taxes but didn't want to pay large fees to get them done. My niche was waiting for me.

In my freshman year, I had taken Accounting 101 and 102. That, plus my enthusiasm and my past as a business kid, were my main qualifications. But how on earth was I going to be a tax preparer with only two courses under my belt? I kept asking myself. The answer came in the form of a suggestion from a friend that I go to H&R Block for Saturday classes.

By the fall of 1982, I had successfully completed the Individual Tax Preparation course and promptly registered a New York sole proprietorship. I was ready for business, and it was with a feeling of excitement that I "put up my shingle."

Having lost none of my flair for the dramatic, I called the outfit L&H Returns Unlimited. My first major test came immediately. *Will I be able to convince a lot of cops that I can do their returns?* I realized that I had to be a more confident and convincing rookie at my new venture than the police rookies I dealt with every day.

Lorna became my soul mate, and she provided not only

emotional support but brought her considerable business acumen to the development of L&H Returns Unlimited. It was as much her decision as mine to invest the first capital we accumulated in acquiring the appropriate technological support for the growing company. She accompanied me to J&R Computers to purchase our first Epson computer. I still recall the thrill of putting in the floppy disks, typing in the DOS commands with their colons and backslashes, then waiting to hear the drives churn slowly inside the machine as it copied my client's tax files one by one. (The sound remains with me as a reminder of the importance of applied technology to successful entrepreneurship.)

As my home-based business grew, so did my confidence in my ability to prepare taxes. I thought we would gain a tremendous advantage if we moved the business to a formal office or major thoroughfare. My business partner Herman DaCosta and I began the quest for a new location. After a few deliberations, we settled in an office shared with a real estate company in the heart of White Plains Road. This brought the added advantage that we could promote ourselves with real estate customers.

Thinking back, I feel as if much of my confidence to launch out in business, while still on the job at the NYPD, came from the sense that I was one of the guys in the department. I really felt welcome and trusted. They even let me carry out a kind of hazing on the rookie cops who came to my section.

"Are you a rookie?" I'd ask each of them as they came in to be outfitted.

"Yes, sir!" came the reply from young men who had been too well drilled to answer in any other way.

"What do you want?" I'd bark.

"Belt, sir!"

"What do you wear—left belt or right belt!?"

"Left belt, sir—"

"You fool!" I'd admonish. "There is no such thing!" One of the rookies who got the treatment stood out among the other fresh faces. The man was one of many blacks who were becoming increasingly attracted to the ranks of the police, but this guy had a kind of British accent—I figured he was Jamaican. The rookie would later tell me he was originally from Redland District in Clarendon, Jamaica, just below Bull Head Mountain.

He had come to New York City at a time when many Caribbean men were arriving in the city and swelling the ranks of the police department. Some had served in Vietnam in the early 1970s while others had fled political violence that badly scarred Jamaica from the mid-1970s to 1980. There was something else about him, though. He didn't seem too fazed by the prank I'd played on him and he was not as green and terrified as the average newcomer to the department. He got his gear and I handed him my business card. He gave me his phone number, and pretty soon he became a regular fixture at home with us in Hillside.

Chance meetings and twists of fate have played a major role in my life. The relationship between Bossville Rhoden and me is the outcome of one such encounter. After our initial meeting, I became his tax accountant and he became my first cop client. Afterward, he began to operate like a marketing agent, directing police rookies to L&H for their tax services. Today, "Boss," my best friend, is happily retired from the NYPD. He operates Golden Krust Franchise #26 at 5 North Main Street in Spring Valley, New York. Each of us is godfather to the other's daughter. Boss has been there for me anywhere, anytime, consulting on security issues, accompanying me to research baking equipment, and even used to accompany me whenever I'd buy a new car. He's an important part of the Franchise Advisory Council and carries the Golden Krust torch well. As will unfold, he has made a profound contribution to the realization of my American Dream.

I decided to specialize in work-related deductions and was willing to do in-home consultations. I advertised by placing fliers all over my lunch room at work, and the client base expanded rapidly. As my business grew, however, I noticed subtle changes in the attitudes of some of my acquaintances. One took to calling me a "brownie" (short for brownnoser). The tingling in my thick skin told me I was getting both admiration and envy from them. And that just spurred me to expand even further. My side business was an open secret. But nobody at the NYPD told me I was doing anything wrong, and the only people who asked about the services were cops who needed them.

CHAPTER EIGHT
Hot Streak

Having passed the five-year mark at the police department, I felt that with the comfort and sense of stability that I had found, I should begin to look for opportunities for my friends and family members to join the ranks of the civil service. By then, I had put in a good word for my tax partner Herman DaCosta, which helped him join the payroll division. My sister-in-law Velma joined the police department's equipment section soon after I had been promoted. I also got my friend Lionel Stewart hired at the Property Clerk's office and a job for my BCC schoolmate Edgar Brown. I was even able to help my sister Jackie get a city agency job. It was like I was building up my own little employment agency.

I had encouraged my wife to take the department test; she passed, and got a job as a police administrative aide. Lorna had good clerical skills, wrote shorthand, and is a great typist, so this was of course the perfect job for her. It meant that she would now be making a lot more money than when she was with the Moravian Church in the city. She would have all the small perks that came with working for the police. My only fear was whether or not she would be able to work around the kind of cops who cursed with every other word they uttered. She once told me, almost in tears, that her superior officer had addressed her using language that is too X-rated for this memoir. The 124 room (the clerical office) at the Bronx's 47th Precinct was no joke, but to her credit, Lorna took on the challenge and handled her job admirably.

Spurred by my good fortune as a freelance accountant, I shoehorned myself into every accounting class I could find on campus. All my electives and extras were dedicated to accounting. If they had allowed it, I would have done my entire degree that way. In 1984, having accumulated sixty credits, I transferred to Baruch College, where the spectacular progress in my academic career was halted. The workload became more challenging, and I had to quickly admit that the going was not as easy as when I was running up the score at Bronx Community College.

I like to call this period in my life one of "qualification accumulation," as I seized every opportunity that presented itself to qualify in every available area of endeavor. No city exam was safe: I took the test for New York Transit motorman, conductor, bus driver, and even the NYPD entry examination itself. Fortunately for the department, I guess, I didn't score highly enough for recruitment into the Police Academy.

My final rush of ambition led me to qualify as a retirement benefit examiner. In retrospect, it seems I must have been engaged in some kind of a game, where I challenged myself to see how well I would score, and perhaps, as a result, find myself in a new and better place in life.

Then, in the fall of 1984, a junior accountant's position became vacant in the New York Police Department's pension section. My superiors encouraged me to do the interview. Turetsky even put in a good word with accounting supervisor Abraham Papelsky and told him what a great guy he'd be getting if they hired me. Things had been flowing so easily for me at the department that I thought I'd be a lock for the job, so I sauntered confidently upstairs to the tenth floor for the interview.

Though I was accustomed to wearing a department uniform shirt and jeans to work, I was now dressed in a new gray suit and tie, expecting the interview to be a formality, just a rubber-stamp affair. There were others up there waiting to apply for accounting and various other administrative positions, but I wasn't fazed by the heavy anxiety that hung over the waiting area.

In turn, I was invited to the interview room, where I faced three people: Inspector Bowden, Kai Ng, and Stanley Jacobis. I extended my hand and thanked them for their time and the opportunity to interview. Soon after I sat down, my attitude quickly turned from self-assuredness to blind panic.

"Do you have a résumé?" Bowden asked.

I thought I was going to be sick. *Wait a second—what résumé? But I'm going to work in the same building . . . you mean I'm not already in?*

"How about your college transcript?" came the follow-up question. I felt blindsided, but I had to be honest and recognize that the other applicants must have had theirs. I was grossly unprepared and my shock reminded me that nothing is a sure thing. I've never been caught off-guard like that again.

Needing sixty-four credits for my associate's degree, I did a late registration at Bronx Community College. A godsend of a biology class made it certain that I'd get over the top with the remaining credit hours I needed. No sooner had the grades hit the computer than I collected my transcript from the college and promptly got the job. It was the first time anyone had hired me full-time as an accountant.

"Forget everything you've learned in school or work," I was told on my first day, as two gigantic brokerage-house reference volumes, covering Commercial Paper & Repurchase Agreements were dropped onto my desk. The books contained details for use in calculating future payments, repurchase agreements, and short-term investments related to police pensions, funds amounting to billions of dollars. It showed what enormous investment power the department had. Awed by my responsibility, I spent months working on maturity dates, repeatedly running permutations of all the ways in which the money could safely multiply.

The promotion brought me more than a bigger paycheck; it gave me stronger credibility as a financial and tax consultant. I felt as if my customers were saying, *This guy's sharp. He knows his stuff.* My confidence received a huge boost too: as a stock handler, I'd worn my department identification card turned inward. When I moved up, I proudly wore it with the title and picture facing out to the world. It may as well have been an advertising sandwich board around my neck with huge graphics at my front and back. What it meant was that my career—and I felt I could now truly call it that—had taken off.

On January 30, 1985, soon after I'd begun working as a pensions accountant at NYPD for the princely sum of $19,000 a year, my grandfather died. I traveled to Jamaica for his funeral, then quickly returned to the States.

Even as I felt the satisfaction from the progress I was making, I reflected on my journey over the last four years of my life in America. The frightened young immigrant, who woke up in the Bronx in May 1981, had overcome a range of challenges to build the foundation on which a dream of successful entrepreneurship could be realized.

Many individuals had contributed to my growth and development. The unqualified support of my parents and their insistence on the primacy of Christian values and family unity was the bedrock that nurtured my confidence and facilitated my progress at all levels. Each of my siblings played their part too, but it was "Mother," with her maternal instincts, who kept all of us in line and demonstrated by example the importance of being there for each other.

Respecting the responsibility of raising two more children after Monique and Daren arrived, I stopped going to classes. At the same time, my business was growing with more accounting clients, and to make things even more complex, I was given additional responsibilities at work. To handle the logistics of jobs and babies, Lorna left the Moravian Church for her job at the 47th Precinct in the Bronx, while I switched to a 6:30 a.m.–2:30 p.m. shift so that I could relieve her with the kids. Fortunately, I became mobile at this time, proudly driving my latest acquisition, a 1978 Datsun 510.

My salary had now grown to $21,000 a year; Lorna's was $18,000. Business had perked up quite a bit too. By 1986, the client list had grown to nearly six hundred. I offered more regular office hours, working 5 p.m.–8 p.m. on Monday, Wednesday, and Saturday. We even introduced mainstream marketing gimmicks, offering twenty dollars to anyone who brought me a new client.

The new business came in fast. Lorna and I began acquiring the symbols of American success. I bought a new Camry while Lorna got herself a Honda Accord. L&H was now a door-to-door service, and I sometimes felt like the traveling broom salesman in Jamaica as I heard kids yelling to their parents, "The tax man is here!" When I showed up, folks just went and got out their shoe boxes full of receipts and papers so I could get to work.

I also felt that I had become a part of mainstream America. My business was expanding and at a personal level, my investment in education together with my success at entrepreneurship had made me far more confident that I'd make my way in the Land of Opportunity.

Through it all, my faith was strengthened as I saw the hand of God in all that I had achieved. Lorna and I became members of the Church of the Nazarene in Valhalla, New York. It was a small, close-knit congregation under the leadership of Pastor Leroy Richards, which held services in a basement rented from the United Methodist Church. There she would enrich the sound of their choir with the beautiful soprano voice she had developed from her earliest years in Jamaica.

Disposable income remained scarce with all we had to purchase, but in the important areas of my life, I felt I was truly on a roll.

Determined to be a minibus driver, a young and ambitious Lowell Hawthorne poses in Kingston on the day he gets his driver's license in March 1977. At the time, he is only sixteen, one year too young to legally drive unsupervised in Jamaica.

Following in his brother Charles's footsteps, Lowell spends his last year of high school at Grantham College in Kingston after attending Oberlin High.

The Hawthorne family home, at left, with the bakery in between the house and the satellite dish with the grocery store at right.

Up to the time Lowell left Jamaica in 1981, there was no running water in Border. This makeshift piping from the local spring was the main source for residents.

The main work area at Hawthorne & Sons Bakery in Border, St. Andrew, Jamaica, in the 1970s. Note the workers kneading and packing dough by hand. Second from the right is Alfred "Maas Feddie" Anderson, whose hand was disfigured in a horrific accident at the bakery.

Lowell and his prized VW 1600 minivan on a typical workday. The bus had no air-conditioning, but he was always cheerful and well dressed for work anyway. On Saturdays, when he ran a bread delivery route to Annotto Bay or Buff Bay (or when he was traveling with his sound system—see photo at right), Lowell would remove the seats to make room. On weekdays, he drove a minibus route from Border and Lawrence Tavern down to Half Way Tree in Kingston. The bus would later become a gift to brother Raymond when Lowell left Jamaica.

May 2, 1981: A teary-eyed group gathers at Kingston's NW Manley Airport. (L–R) Densford Clarke, Ainsworth Henry, Lowell, Burnett "Garvey" Morrison, Frederick Hawthorne (Lowell's cousin and minibus sideman), Raymond Hawthorne, and niece Nataki. Lowell was about to leave behind his entire business and primary social network for the unknown.

At the NYPD on Lowell's twenty-second birthday. L–R: Officer Donald McNeil, Thomas Lutanya, Lowell, and Sergeant Marty Turetsky.

Al Alston (right) with Lowell and Louis Dory (center) in the NYPD's accounting department at Police Plaza. Alston would become director of franchise development at Golden Krust and later claim the 100th GK franchise when his store opened in Queens, New York.

This 1989 photo shows the original Gun Hill Road location in the Bronx (at center left) opposite the number 5 subway entrance. In time, this would become the nerve center of Golden Krust. The brand amassed so much goodwill that many visitors seeking the shop would cross the street from the station and head for the more impressive New York Public Library (at center right). The librarians had to constantly redirect people to GK's more modest building with its tiny parking lot. Just inside the lot is the delivery van which had previously been an undercover police vehicle.

Van number 6 of Golden Krust's six-vehicle fleet, c.1990. As a tribute to the origins of the business, the vehicles proudly display the phrase: *By Hawthorne & Sons.*

In the early days at Gun Hill Road, Lowell and best friend, ex-cop Bossville "Boss" Rhoden, baked the goods, manned the registers, and made deliveries. Here, they take a moment in a hectic day for reflection.

Not yet a franchise operation, Golden Krust expanded its product sales through neighborhood food stores that served as agencies of the brand.

While saving money to buy their first house, Lowell and Lorna (front) have their 1985 wedding reception at sister Lauris "Mother" Hawthorne's home at 3340 Corso Avenue in the Bronx. Lorna is wearing sister Paulette's (left) wedding dress.

The Rock Cliff Hotel in Negril, Jamaica. A picturesque hideaway at the westernmost end of the island, the hotel was the scene of the most difficult business decisions ever made in the life of Golden Krust.

Riding high on the success of a growing business, Lowell and Lorna (right) ham it up for the camera on vacation in Negril. At center is sister Cassandra Hawthorne; at rear, niece Marcia. Within hours, devastating news from New York signaled looming disaster for Golden Krust.

Friends, family, employees, and officials crowd into the Park Avenue facility for the official opening in November 1993.

Golden Krust manufacturing plant and corporate office, located at 3958 Park Avenue in the Bronx.

Mama and Pops stand proudly with Lowell at Golden Krust's new USDA plant on Park Avenue in the Bronx, November 1993.

Mel, the guru of Golden Krust's patty-meat formula. In all the years he worked for GK, he never revealed his secrets to the company. Lowell, who originally traveled to Jamaica to find Mel, coax him out of retirement, and bring him to New York, would later have to devise his own recipe.

Golden Krust patties successfully entered the supermarket and shopping club channels. By 2010, the product was also available in four varieties for the microwave.

Former Prime Minister of Jamaica, the Honorable P.J. Patterson was on hand to celebrate the grand opening of Golden Krust's 100th store. Mr. Patterson is pictured making a presentation to Lowell and Jacqueline Hawthorne-Robinson as Lorraine Hawthorne-Morrison observes the happy moment in the background (*top*).

At the celebration service to mark Golden Krust's 20th anniversary, several clergy members lay hands on the Hawthorne founders and family, praying for God's continued blessing (*center*).

Lowell and Lorna are all smiles as they celebrate Lowell's joyous reception of the Order of Distinction from his native Jamaica (*left*).

An elated Lowell Hawthorne collects the 2010 *Jamaica Observer* Business Leader Award from *Observer* Chairman Gordon "Butch" Steward at a glitzy awards ceremony held at the Jamaica Pegasus Hotel in Kingston. Mr. Hawthorne won from a field of eight nominees from the Jamaican Diaspora.

On what he has called "one of the proudest days of my life," Lowell Hawthorne is invested with the Commander of the Order of Distinction by Jamaica's Governor-General Sir Howard Cooke on National Heroes Day, October 2005.

On the day the 100th GK franchise location opens, Prime Minister of Jamaica, the Most Honorable P.J. Patterson, accepts a special Golden Krust Award of Appreciation from the Golden Krust CEO in 2005.

In the early days of the company, Lowell would sometimes travel in disguise to observe rival operations and test the competition's product.

Roughly twenty years after leaving his minibus dreams behind in Jamaica, Lowell is featured in a New York transit advertising campaign as a graduate and benefactor of the City University of New York.

In aid of the Golden Krust Foundation's scholarship efforts, the company launches its Pennies for Change Campaign in 2005, aimed at collecting loose change at Golden Krust locations all over the U.S.

A bakery conveyor takes Golden Krust patties from pie line to oven in 2007.

As he has been since the early days, Lowell "The Patty King" is still involved in day-to-day operations.

After years of evolution and modernization, the Golden Krust restaurant interior is as inviting as ever.

Lowell proudly displays his honorary Doctor of Letters degree at the ceremony in the Founders Auditorium at Medgar Evers College in September 2011.

In honor of the late Ephraim Hawthorne, workers at the Bronx manufacturing facility place a chair outside the main ovens in March of 2007, the first time he was absent at springtime. Pops traditionally visited the plant for the start of Easter bun production and sat in this warm spot waiting to inspect the first batches.

From left to right, sons Omar and Daren, daughter Monique, wife Lorna, Lowell, and eldest son Haywood.

Papa, the patriarch, with Mama (top right) and Ms. Pat (top left), who he married after Mama's death in 1994. Below are generations of Hawthorne children, and at bottom, the eleven Hawthorne siblings, from left: Lloyd, Raymond, Leroy, Charles, Lowell, Milton, Lauris, Novlet, Jacqueline, Lorraine, and Cassandra.

The Golden Krust founders, clockwise from left: Jackie, Lloyd, Lorna, Lowell, Lauris ("Mother"), Milton, and Velma.

CHAPTER NINE
Golden Krust Is Born

My ambition to carve out a niche for myself in corporate America drove me in the direction of professional and academic certification. My immediate goal was to become a New York State Certified Public Accountant. I had left Bronx Community College with sixty-four credits in accounting and business which was a fair achievement, but not nearly enough for the greater sense of fulfillment that I sought. I was motivated and mentally ready to pursue my professional career more avidly. Alas, I only lasted two semesters at Baruch College. In order to be closer to home and the business in the Bronx, I transferred to Lehman College.

By 1989, after eight years at the NYPD, I began to feel a stronger urge to go into business on my own full time. Except for my first year in the United States, I had always operated my own little business and made a profit. The accounting business had grown to the point where I needed additional staff and had taken on Kai Ng and Al Alston, both civilians at the department, as my right-hand guys.

Still, the urge to engage in full-time entrepreneurship became increasingly intense with every increment of success in my accounting business. I had started earning enough to acquire one of the first portable briefcase phones—state of the art at that time—which allowed me to make and take business calls without using the department's lines. I did not see my accounting business, however, as the full-time enterprise that would satisfy my entrepreneurial drive; my mind kept on going back to Border and the family bakery.

Gradually, with three evenings a week at the tax office, I was trying to give another full measure of my commitment to L&H and its ever-growing clientele. I had spent five years in the equipment section at the police department without calling in sick even once. I was reliable, punctual, disciplined, and respectful.

These were the attributes that made me an exemplary member of the NYPD staff. My work ethic, along with the aggressive marketing of my accounting services to police personnel, brought me respect in police circles and earned me a reputation of trustworthiness which I enjoy to this day. Such was the mark that I made at the NYPD, I'm told, that many newspaper articles trumpeting my later business and community successes would be posted on the bulletin boards at police headquarters!

The global economy of the twenty-first century, with its rapid technological advancements and crucial information demands, will place an ever-growing emphasis on education for successful competition. Over time, I've learned that while academic certification is not a guarantee for entrepreneurial success, education is vital, especially in franchising. My experiences and setbacks provided valuable training for my path, but for all my blessings, including God-given talents and the help of a great many people, I could never have become qualified to be the CFO of my company without my core business education.

During my last several months at the NYPD, other members of the Hawthorne family moved from Jamaica to the U.S. The bakery back in Border had begun to scale down operations as competition from both local and imported baked goods into the Jamaican market made the family business less profitable. Pops found it more beneficial at Easter to operate a bun business in "Mother's" basement than to get bogged down with Easter buns in Jamaica and miss being able to spend time with us. By 1987, he was producing between one to two hundred units each season. At fifty-nine, Papa had lost none of his entrepreneurial drive.

The thought of getting involved in Papa's venture not only crossed my mind, but was soon consuming my thinking. One immediate constraint was that Easter, the peak time for the bun market, was also tax season, the busiest for L&H as we handled my clients' annual tax returns. Still, the prospect of a family business on American soil became increasingly irresistible.

With the benefit of hindsight, I now see even more clearly that Golden Krust was not born out of a single-spark event or a "big bang" moment. It simply came together over time—and at the right time. By now, many family members had migrated to America and lived within easy access of each other. Papa's experiment with Easter buns had demonstrated the potential for a full-fledged bakery. It didn't take long for the synergies of the family to come together around an activity that was always in our blood.

"We all did this business in Jamaica," I remember saying excitedly on the phone to Boss one day. "Of course it can work! If I get one hundred pounds of flour, so much water, sugar, and other ingredients, I can bake some bread, quickly turn it over, buy more raw material . . ." With each passing day, the idea of establishing a family bakery dominated my thoughts. Things went on that way until it felt as if the work I discussed on the phone had completely overtaken the work I was doing in the police pensions section.

One day, as I walked out of Police Plaza to answer my cell phone out of NYPD earshot, it dawned on me that while I had given the department a lot of good, honest work, L&H was becoming too high profile and it was time for me to voluntarily move on.

Although I knew I would have to come to a parting of ways with the NYPD, it was still a hard decision for me to quit a job I had kept for over nine years without a clear plan as to how I would provide for my family of six, and tend to other obligations that could come to the fore.

My next step was to call the members of the family to a meeting. Although the entire family could not attend, I was happy to gather with Lorna, my siblings "Mother," Jacqueline, Milton, Lloyd, my sister-in law Velma, Papa, and my best friend Boss. As much as I would have preferred all of my siblings to have been with us that evening, the fact was that some were still living in Jamaica, others had not yet expressed strong interest in the bakery business, and a few felt that an investment at that time was beyond their means.

I remember that Sunday evening we were all sitting around in the living room at Mickle Avenue having enjoyed the great meal Lorna had prepared for the group. Boss, my siblings, and my in-laws occupied all the chairs and several spots on the floor. It was in this environment that Papa challenged the family with a far-reaching question.

"What if we set up a little place?" he asked the group. The idea of a family enterprise in New York resonated with all of us. As always, he was on the mark and once again demonstrated the enormous power of his ideas which were always so simple, decisive, and effective.

Before the night was out, we all agreed to establish the family bakery in America, simply to supply the local West

Indian community and our friends as we had done in Jamaica. That was the extent of our plan at that first meeting. It was informal and only moderately ambitious, a far cry from the current Golden Krust vision "to take the taste of the Caribbean to the world."

Even with this limited objective, I knew that it would require a special effort from me to keep the family team focused on the goal of making a Hawthorne bakery in America a success. I would still have to find the time to push hard with my part-time business, since the revenue, although seasonal, had become an important part of the income on which my wife and kids depended.

Having taken the decision to invest, our next step was to raise the required capital. At the same time, I would have to ensure that whatever was done wouldn't jeopardize the financial viability of my siblings' and friends' families. Such was my enthusiasm for the project that soon I took the unprecedented step of seeking a bank loan. So I got into the commercial line at a local bank to apply for funding to set up the business. Just as quickly, I was directed to the Small Business Administration (SBA) to try my luck. I seem to recall the banker expressing the view that "the restaurant business carries a high risk factor." My application was rejected.

The SBA people were polite, but as soon as they asked for my nonexistent business plan and informed me of all the paperwork that would be required, I knew we would not find seed funds in any such financial institution. I was almost ready to quit when I reported to the family, "Guys, it doesn't look good . . ." They knew it as well as I did. The only solution to the financing problem was for us to mortgage our lives in the service of the cause.

As the only homeowners among us at the time, both

"Mother" and I put our homes up as collateral. The others emptied their savings accounts or borrowed as best they could. We would not be denied. I got one of Boss's brother officers at the NYPD to lend me $5,000 for twelve months at 20 percent interest to help fund the business (one year to the day, I repaid the loan on time with the agreed interest). By the time we were finished pooling funds from every source, the family had raised $107,000.

The next step was to find a location from which to operate. After months of searching, we finally found one on Gun Hill Road in the Bronx. We began the work of navigating a virtual cobweb of city codes to get the permits for moving the business forward.

We had actually formed the corporation in 1988 and had named all the directors at that time. The lease was signed in February 1989 and once this was done, I immediately pushed to secure permits and everything required to get the business up and running. High on our list of priorities was hiring an architectural firm to have all the necessary blueprints drawn up.

During this extremely busy period, I still had my job at One Police Plaza, but it had become clear to me that getting the store ready before the lease commencement would require my full-time attention.

With a thriving tax business and a lease in hand, I began to contemplate the unthinkable—quitting the job that had been the basis of my family's security for more than nine years. This was not an easy decision for me, especially since I had a wife, four children, and other responsibilities as well. Such a decision could only be taken after a serious discussion with Lorna. Of course, just as any other wife might be, she was very concerned about my desire to give up steady long-term income. As we sat and talked, however, we were able to sketch out a plan to ensure that even with our new business obligations, we would still be able to pay the piper.

Having embraced the idea and having come to grips with the fact that for me to achieve my entrepreneurial goals I would need to take a leave of absence from my day job at the NYPD, I decided that a discussion with both of my bosses—Abraham Papilsky and the commanding officer, Inspector Philip Bowden, and chief of the police pension section—could not be delayed. Despite having worked for over nine years at the NYPD, I had never been inside Bowden's office. That made me more than a little nervous, now that I had such a big request to make. I meekly knocked on the door.

"Inspector, can I see you?" I inquired.

"Sure you can," he replied. I went in, took a seat, and looked straight ahead. I had planned to keep the conversation very brief, not knowing how he would take the unusual request I was sure would stick in my throat.

"Sir," I began, "my wife has already taken a leave of absence after the birth of our first two children. She's just had a third and I believe it's my time to stay home with my young son Daren."

"Really? And how long are you looking to stay home for?"

"Two to three years," I said, "unless circumstances change."

I could hardly believe my luck when the inspector said he would not take issue with this. I immediately notified all the other supervisors in the pensions division of my decision. As far as I was concerned, the most important thing I had achieved was that I would still be able to return to my job if the business venture tanked.

I also had eight weeks of accumulated sick leave, so I

applied for that too. Accounting Supervisor Papelsky read me the Riot Act.

"I can send a squad car to your house," he told me menacingly, "to make sure you're really sick!" I'd pushed my luck too far.

In that moment, I was sure I could no longer continue as a police pensions accountant. Despite all the time spent in class getting qualifications, I now knew I wasn't going to be a tax accountant. I was also certain that after my special leave ended, so would my NYPD career. The family bakery idea wouldn't wait.

Many of the professionals I worked with at the NYPD thought that it was a bad idea to give up a good city job to start a bakery business. They saw a patty as only a snack, while I saw the enterprise as an opportunity to make millions selling a popular food staple. In one of my discussions with Kai Ng, I asked him to calculate what my retirement benefits would be if I were to wait for the additional months of service I'd need to qualify.

His answer was an eye-opener. Based on his calculations, all I would start receiving thirty-five years later would be $90 a month! That was all I needed to hear. I had no intention of staying on for three critical months just to qualify for a $90 pension—while missing the opportunity of a lifetime. I continued to work at NYPD while simultaneously sorting out the logistics and putting plans in place for the start-up of the business. As it came closer to our launch date, I had my boss sign the leave form. I can still remember the caption on the letter:

MILITARY AND EXTENDED LEAVE OF ABSENCE FOR
CHILD CARE.

It certainly gave me the assurance and the confidence to go forth and get the bakery started.

Even before the decision was taken to establish the enterprise, family members were already acquiring talents that the business would need, particularly the critical marketing skills we all developed selling our quota of Easter buns each spring. Velma and Boss at the NYPD, Jackie at the bank, Charles on the LIU campus, and "Mother" at the nursing home were already selling Papa's buns to their colleagues. My oldest brother Lloyd also had a good following of transplanted Jamaicans.

At the start, my place at the head of the company was not predetermined. As the sixth of eleven siblings, I hardly expected to be first in line. What gave me some leverage was the fact that I had a viable business and owned a home, two facts that meant that I'd be making the biggest sacrifice and contributing most of the initial capital required. The fact that I was the first to commit my assets to the venture raised my leadership profile. Then my role as the accountant on the flow chart, together with the firm backing of my eldest sibling, "Mother," finally sealed the issue. I would be CEO.

Still, persuading everyone to risk so much of what they had in a business venture took some effort. Once viability was established, however, Milton quit his job at Ford Motor Company, Jackie left the bank, "Mother" gave up both her jobs, while Lloyd resigned from a prominent U.S.-Jamaican food company. Finally, Velma and Lorna, who by now were both administrators at the NYPD, turned in their resignations as well.

There were still many details to be worked out, but the unity of the family around this critical project was eloquent testimony to the success of Papa and Mama's nurturing. It was also confirmation that we had a good foundation on which to build.

At the outset, I predicted that given our tight budget we would never be able to hire the staff required for either the bakery or sales departments.

Available family members were asked to carry the load; they all responded in the affirmative. Those who were not able to finalize separation from their jobs immediately came in part-time to get the shop going. Soon, there were enough of us living in the city to fill the key slots. We took just enough salary for living expenses at first and bought only old or used equipment. Our hiring strategy for our first set of outside employees—which included Moses Richards, who is still with the company, and David Seymour—was archaic; it was a semi-bartering agreement where they gave their labor for a promise of future employment. Nonetheless, there was an inspiring energy about the whole thing.

With all the goodwill and enthusiasm in the air, it was still a very tall order at the start to make a good product, get the word out, fulfill all our financial obligations, and generate enough profit to sustain the family. There was also one other small problem. Baked goods aimed at the West Indian market included coco bread, corn bread, duck bread, and gizzada (spicy grated coconut baked into a small, hard pastry shell), which were items Hawthorne & Sons had made back in Jamaica. All these products combined, however, paled in comparison to the sales of Jamaican patties in the target market. And we had no idea how to make a really good commercial Jamaican patty.

Originally, Jamaican patties were a kind of flaky turnover filled with spicy meat, traditionally beef. For the uninitiated, the product is a simple, perfectly self-contained, well-balanced meal that is inexpensive and accessibly priced for a wide market. Today, there is more variety with fillings such as steamed vegetables, callaloo, fish, ackee, soy, shrimp, chicken, and cheese. In New York's Latino neighborhoods, the Jamaican patty is called an *empanada* in honor of a similar Spanish food of that name.

The consistency of the crust and flavor of the filling are so specific that to this day, there are not many large commercial patty manufacturers either in Jamaica or the United States. In Jamaica, there are only three or four; in America, a mere handful exists. For people in the food business, it's easier to buy good patties wholesale and re-sell them at a small profit than to manucafture them from scratch. All the makers, however, are only too aware of the risks involved in maintaining consistency. If the crust is made too thick and dry; if the filling is not within the expected range of flavor; or if the finished product leaks before it can even be bitten into, you'll be laughed out of business. I remember Mama and Papa making a homemade version of the patty to fill special orders for customers and friends. Theirs were okay, but would never be the kind of culture-shaping product that came out of places like Tastee and Bruce's in Kingston. Our bakery in Border made most of its revenue from bread, bun, and bulla. By contrast, the patty bakeries in Kingston, which had been around since the 1960s, were cash factories with secret recipes and loyal fans all over. Cash-strapped, we were without sufficient equipment, staff, or store furnishings—definitely not one of those specialty bakeries.

Several family meetings followed, in which we tried to hammer out operational details concerning location, products, a suitable company name, and job descriptions. These early days were full of a strong can-do spirit, as well as an abiding faith in our family and in God. Our gatherings were marked by a heartfelt desire to work hard and succeed, but also to explore and learn as much as we could while subjecting ourselves to Divine guidance.

The division of labor practically decided itself. Milton, given his technical background, was the obvious choice to fill the engineering and technology slot; Jackie would be the general manager and a "jack of all trades"; Lorna, who had worked in personnel at the NYPD, became our human resources director; Lloyd was an experienced baker; Velma was responsible for pastries and cakes, routinely tantalizing us all with her baked treats; big sister "Mother," a fabulous cook, was our first chef; Raymond managed the bakery; Charles, the math brain, spent many hours in the library doing demos that would help us run important financial projections; my niece Desrene was sales director; my sisters Lorraine and Cassandra handled the books; my accounting partners, Herman, Kai, and Al, were given the task of procuring the appropriate licenses for the establishment of a bakery; Boss and I searched for an ideal spot to set up business; the other siblings and in-laws pitched in wherever help was needed to get the business up and running. Because of my financial background, I started out as both the chief financial and chief executive officer.

As we pondered the idea of self-employment, Lorna and I thought it was important to ensure we could continue to pay our mortgage and take care of family without a steady paycheck. We turned to the only option available: we hired Samuel Menns to convert the first-floor apartment of our two-family Bronx home into a two-bedroom suite to be rented. This allowed us to cover the mortgage, and it was one headache we no longer had to worry about.

The name Golden Krust emerged through a suggestion from our real estate agent, Godfrey Wallace, following a long discussion of who we really were, as well as the unique and flavorful products we were making. Certainly we had not thought about intellectual property rights and ownership of the brand before beginning to print business cards, packaging, and signage. This would come to complicate matters later on.

Truth be told, Papa and I would have been satisfied using some version of "Hawthorne & Sons Bakery" for our new entity, and if I could have foreseen the trials the company would endure as a result of our choice of name, we certainly would have used the family name instead.

Finding an ideal location for the bakery proved to be a major challenge. Food and drink brands like Chock full o'Nuts had done well in New York by locating their shops near subway entrances and street corners to maximize pedestrian traffic. This was the strategy we sought to emulate as we searched the tri-state area for the best location. We also wanted a spot that not only had high traffic and high visibility, but was also a place where West Indian customers could find us without too much effort. We looked for options all over the Bronx that would fit the bill—Eastchester, Grand Concourse, White Plains Road, and others—but in the end Boss and I chose a perfect location, a property at 1381 East Gun Hill Road.

Our intention from the start was to acquire title to the building. We entered into a contract with a real estate broker on Gun Hill Road for the purchase. The price was originally quoted at $335,000. After two months of failure to secure a mortgage, the owner cancelled the deal, saying we'd have to rent the building if we wanted to use it. Knowing he had us over a barrel, he proposed to keep our

$26,000 deposit as rental security and charge us $2,800 a month in rent. "Buy it or lose it," he told us, "make a decision." Reluctantly, but without a choice, we agreed to the terms and were forced to start out in the building as lessees, not owners. We retained the right of first refusal to purchase the property.

The location suited us, and so despite the challenges with the acquisition, we finally assumed full ownership in 1992. To this day, it still galls me to think of the way the seller took advantage of our predicament. Predictably, Papa had been consistent in his view that despite the inflated cost, our best option was to "pay him his money and get rid of him."

Getting the place ready for business was another tedious process characterized by trial and error. Our experience in establishing and operating businesses in Jamaica hardly prepared us for the range of operational issues and regulations which were a part of the process in New York. The food handling permits, the waste disposal issues, and insurance alone made my head spin. These were the same issues that confronted my niece Desrene and my sister Lorraine years later when they prepared the tedious documentation for our franchise license. The process required a great deal of time and persistence to navigate the maze of red tape.

No group of highly paid staffers could have worked as hard as my voluntary staff did to get things going. Milton and Lloyd did much of the early construction over the three or four months it took to get the building legally ready for on-site manufacturing and retail.

Finding the right equipment that was affordable and which produced our particular product line proved very difficult at the outset. Because of import restrictions from

Jamaica, we sometimes had to scramble to find some things. Jamaican bread is so unique that we had to bring in a dough-breaking equipment from the island to give it that special texture. It took a kind of stubborn faith, but faith nonetheless, for us to slowly roll forward. After four months of painstaking work, sleepless nights, anxiety, trepidation, and uncertainties, we finally obtained most of our licenses to start doing business.

On the night before we opened for the first time, we were all there just like in the old days at Border, only this time the family was totally involved in the baking. The aroma of freshly baked hardo bread, spice bun, bulla, coco bread (that wonderful bread envelope designed to hold a patty), and other Caribbean delights like coconut drops, grater cake, and our famous rum cake blanketed the entire building.

As the first items came off the line, the entire family erupted in celebratory cheers and gave thanks to God for bringing us this far. Once again, we experienced the truth expressed in Papa's favorite verse from the Bible: *We know that all things work together for good to them that love the Lord and to them who are called according to His purpose.*

We then turned to the final preparations for opening day. Everyone pitched in, regardless of skill set or job title. We got ten food display cases and shelving for the store's front area, and stocked them with as many items as we could bake using the small oven space available to us. We also decided to buy wholesale patties from another bakery in New York which sold a tried and tested product. We felt that theirs would work for us as well.

At ten o'clock the next morning we opened the doors and waited. All of us were lined up at the counter, facing the door. Our welcoming committee was a little nervous, but it didn't take long before a woman named Mavis walked in the door and made the first purchase. Relieved and enormously proud, we all clapped and cheered as one by one, the hungry and the curious got off the number 5 subway, crossed East Gun Hill Road, and came in the door. We did three to four hundred dollars in sales that first day. Golden Krust was finally off to a good start.

The company was lucky enough to inherit its first delivery vehicle, an old brown Chevy van that Boss's dad had given him. Ironically, the vehicle had also served as Boss's undercover van in his plainclothes days at the NYPD, when he and other colleagues in Narcotics had often used it on drug buys and busts all over the map.

As we would discover, however, there would be many frustrations and challenges before Golden Krust would find its true rhythm.

When we started to finalize contracts for the new services we would need, garbage removal was highest on our list. But even before contacting any of the service providers we had identified, a sequence of events unfolded that would open our eyes to the stern realities of doing business in New York.

I'd heard of the Mafia, the Syndicate, organized crime. Growing up in Jamaica, there wasn't much talk about the American mob—except what we saw in the movies—and the way they had infiltrated and controlled certain industries in parts of the United States since the early 1900s. I'd heard of them, I just never expected I'd be doing business with them in New York City.

Our first encounter with a "crime family" happened on the day my family opened for business in August 1989. As I recall, nobody was present when the shop was branded by the garbage collectors who "controlled the neighborhood." Their tactics were simple: first, someone placed a decal on our front door indicating the name of the carting company that serviced the route that included our address. Then there was a verbal message left with one of my sisters.

"I need to see the boss," the man said, "so I'll come back tomorrow."

A dumpster was soon dropped off outside the building, without even a discussion with us about establishing garbage disposal service.

As soon as I heard about it, I knew that this visitation was ominous. I also felt that the strain on our cash flow would be significant, especially since we had not yet made our first dollar of profit. At that time, my faith in God was not as strong as it is today, as I had not yet accepted the Lord as my personal Savior and therefore did not pray as fervently as I should have for a way out.

The meeting finally took place. I remember standing outside the store, flanked by Lloyd and Jackie. Facing us were two men, obviously father and son. The whole encounter was short, simple, and to the point, lasting no more than a few minutes.

"We've been the carting company that controls ten square miles in the Bronx," the older man said, "including your shop. We'll be your garbage collectors."

"Is there a way we can compare prices with other carting companies?" I asked, still hanging on to some notion that I was in a reasonable business negotiation.

The younger man looked at me like I'd taken leave of my senses. "This is our territory," he snapped, "and nobody else comes here. Your fee will be $350 a week, paid every Tuesday—and it must be paid in cash. We don't accept checks . . ."

Just imagine: we hadn't yet made a dime, but there we were, staring down a couple of extortionists on a sidewalk in the Bronx.

As far as we could figure, there was just nothing that could be done. So we accepted the devil's deal and began paying these people for carting. Business started rolling, and we soon had a slight increase in trash volume. Within six weeks we were told that our rate would go up to $550 per week. *Two hundred dollars more—after only a few weeks? Ridiculous.*

The situation was dire, especially since law enforcement at the time rarely got involved in this type of situation. Outraged, I called Boss to see how the police department might tackle the problem. After months of investigation by him, we realized that there was not much that we could do about this carting company. Whether we liked it or not, they planned to be with us permanently, like expensive old luggage.

By the end of 1991, our second year of operation, we were paying $1,500 a week. We literally now had wiseguys on our payroll. "Mother," Jackie, and Lorna would ensure that an envelope was prepared in time for pickup every Tuesday. And as we saw each Tuesday approach, we feared what kind of consequences there might be if we didn't have our payment ready.

Perhaps it was the stress, but through this experience I truly felt as if I was being drawn closer to the Lord. Regardless of the successes or disappointments we experienced, our choice was to make Christ the center and joy of our lives.

Business was booming, and in time, Lorna and I moved fifteen miles north of the Bronx to White Plains, Westchester County, two years after the birth of Golden Krust. The

change was meant to allow us to raise our children in sub-
urbs that were safer than our Bronx neighborhood and had
a better school system. This was important for us since we
now had four kids and were also responsible for the welfare of nieces and nephews.

Our new small town of just over 50,000 was mostly
white, with middle-and upper-class families. The seat of
government for Westchester, White Plains is also the center for corporate and retail activity in the area, with peace-
ful, green spaces just twenty-five miles from Manhattan.
This was great for us, because we knew we could have
more indoor and outdoor room for the family while still
being reasonably close to work.

The house we chose was a four-bedroom beauty sitting on a third of an acre. The property had an enormous
backyard that proved irresistible to my parents and other
family members who often used it for cookouts, family re-
unions, and private events. Although we enjoyed the home,
however, Lorna and I had many days of concern, knowing
that our front yard actually faced Route 100A, the main
thouroughfare that joins major intersections in the area.
Imagine having four small children with bikes, tricycles,
and toys playing where the house literally borders a high-
way. Lorna and I found ourselves giving frequent household lectures about the dangers of traffic.

We also had to make adjustments to our definitions of
convenience. There was no neighborhood grocery of the kind
we knew; corner shops like the ones we saw so plentiful and
close together in the Bronx were nowhere to be found.

Acclimating was also slow in coming. Unlike when
we lived in the Bronx and had nearly all our relatives and
friends within easy reach, we didn't know anyone in our
new neighborhood. In time, however, Lorna forged sev-

eral local relationships, and eventually joined the Caribbean American Club. That organization yielded some good
contacts and allowed us to initiate more than a few lasting
friendships.

It was during this period that I began attending Bible
classes and prayer meetings in White Plains at the home
of the Reverend Leroy Richards. After several sessions of
inspiration and blessing, I became increasingly drawn to
the Gospel and gave my heart to the Lord.

In November of 1993, I was baptized at Bronx Bethany
Church of the Nazarene, sister church to what was the
newly formed First Community Church of the Nazarene
in White Plains. My mother rejoiced. I'll never forget that
Sunday afternoon at East 227th Street in the Bronx, when
Pastors Cole and Richards held my hand and declared, "I
now baptize you in the name of the Father, the Son, and
the Holy Ghost." With the words still ringing in my ears,
Pastor Richards immersed me in the water. I emerged re-
born. Although my father, brothers, sisters, and many to
whom I was closest had been praying with us during our
Mafia crisis, these two ministers were special in giving me
so much attention, even though I had only known them for
a year or two.

I credit my good friend Arlene Nembhard with getting
me to those first meetings at Pastor Richards's home in
White Plains. Without her urging, I may never have accepted salvation, which has molded my character, and has
given me the assurance of faith and hope that is a part of
everything I do. Deep down, I still divide my life between
everything that occurred before that moment and everything since . . .

Having embraced Christ as my personal Savior, received the water baptism and the assurance of the abiding

presence of God through the filling of the Holy Ghost, I had renewed vigor and determination, and I felt I was ready to take on anything.

By this point, Golden Krust was paying in excess of $7,000 a month to get rid of the garbage we generated. It was clear that we would never be able to keep paying this escalating bill and stay in business. So one week, wearing God's armor and with the support of my friends, I decided not to pay the wiseguys. Boss made sure we completely broke neighborhood tradition by getting quotes from potential new carriers that very week.

Our faith would be severely tested. We arrived at work that Thursday morning and were greeted with an odor so foul, it soiled the air all along our stretch of Gun Hill Road as far as Eastchester Road. What we discovered next was right out of Hollywood: rotting fish parts and fishy water had been dumped all over the street near our premises. I recall that soon afterward, I got on the prayer banner with my pastors who began to pray with me. Pastor Cole asked me to come to Bronx Bethany to testify about my life as a Christian businessman.

At that Easter Sunday service, I asked the church to pray for us with the hope that God would make a way out of the situation we were facing. The guys working in the bakery had been gracious enough to tackle cleaning and sanitizing the areas affected by the stench. But as much as we scrubbed and made everything fresh again, we couldn't erase the fear we felt, and seeing the younger of the two garbage mobsters coming back every week to collect his fees certainly didn't help. We knew this was no movie— these were guys who might just up and burn your business down. But Boss was tenacious under threat. He brought in a new garbage contractor and we stood our ground.

Despite the danger we must have been in at the time, we refused to give in. Our new carting service stayed in place. Weeks and months of speculation and trepidation passed, with no clear end to the standoff in sight.

Then, in late 1993, a breath of anti-Mafia air blew through New York. Former U.S. Attorney Rudolph Giuliani was elected the city's first Republican mayor since the 1960s. He brought with him a reputation for fearlessly prosecuting the heads of the notorious Five Families of the New York Mafia and later, the insider trading cases on Wall Street.

Targeting quality-of-life crimes, Giuliani did much to clear the mob out of the Fulton Fish Market, and under his administration, a publicly traded carting company, Waste Management Inc., was able to gain a powerful stake in the New York garbage business.

Our prayers were answered: Golden Krust's former self-appointed garbage contractors stopped coming around. Under the new setup, our carting fees had fallen from $7,000 a month to $1,500. Best of all, the new contractors extended us credit and accepted company checks. Gaining freedom from the mob's grip had taken us almost four years.

Thank God we survived the ordeal with very little incident.

CHAPTER TEN
Opportunity Amid Crisis

O ur decision to purchase patties to sell along with our bread and buns impacted our revenues substantially. The sale of 5,000 one-dollar patties a week generated 40 percent of Golden Krust's revenue. It hadn't hurt that the growing West Indian population in the Bronx often seemed to come out of the number 5 subway station all at once and cross Gun Hill Road to buy baked goods at Golden Krust before going home. With very little advertising, the bakery quickly became a genuine household name. We didn't need market research yet to confirm this. During the first couple years of Golden Krust, we simply took careful note of the growing number of out-of-state license plates that came onto Gun Hill Road to buy our wares. Folks were literally coming in from all over.

We knew we had a golden opportunity to spread the reach of the brand. As a means of expanding rapidly, we reached out to various individuals to buy shares in an individual corporation where Golden Krust would remain the major shareholder.

At one point, we also formed a partnership with Donald Smith who had owned at least three bakeries and was doing business as Golden Krust/Caribbean Choice. In fact, during the time before we got our franchising license, we had several individuals who were operating under the GK umbrella, enjoying high revenues. What was important to us at the time was to build the brand by creating that "billboard effect" at all costs by having as many Golden Krust awnings as possible visible within the tri-state area.

This creative mode of doing business paved the way for us once we decided it was time to become a franchise business. Sadly, many of these subsidiaries, partnerships, and other unorthodox relationships did not last once we became a franchisor. Many of the individuals involved had no interest in being part of a concept that required a formal process that included franchise fees. Many parted company with us as the business moved to the next level.

Friends wanted to get in on the action, and so we decided to extend the reach of the business by expanding into Mt. Vernon at 67 South 4th Avenue. Then we set up two other locations, partnerships at Fulton and Nostrand Avenues and 931 Flatbush in Brooklyn. This made for a total of thirteen stores and subsidiaries, including those in Paterson (New Jersey), Flatbush (Brooklyn) and Parsons Boulevard (Queens), as well as Hillside Avenue (Queens). This hodgepodge of outlets emerged without any master location plan or branding blueprint. For all I knew, having the name Golden Krust on the signs above these places meant they traded on the popularity of our flagship at Gun Hill. It didn't guarantee, however, that they'd sell any particular proportion of GK goods as compared to others. But that wasn't a problem for us, at least not yet.

All the same, everything was going extremely well, and we were able to meet our obligations and pay family staff. Just as I had done when I was a minibus operator in Jamaica, I got the urge to take a vacation as soon as there was a little extra money and a little extra time to enjoy it. Lorna and I decided to go with other family members to the pure white sands of Negril at the westernmost tip of Jamaica. At that time, Negril was still relatively underdeveloped, a place where clean little lean-to buildings often served as cabins for grateful visitors eager to enjoy the unspoiled beauty of the legendary beach.

Although the business had been expanding, there wasn't enough money to stay at the finest hotels when we vacationed on the island. Usually, we stayed with family and friends. This time we arrived in Kingston and visited with our circle of family and connections there. Then I was back in minibus mode, loading everyone up to drive across the island to Negril. For that leg of the vacation, I wanted to do something special, so I made contact with my brother-in-law Vincent Clarke, general manager at Jamaica's hardware giant, Rapid Sheffield. Having been the chief supplier during the construction of Rock Cliff Hotel, he used his contacts to secure a special rate for us with the hotel's owners, allowing us to secure two rooms at a discounted rate.

I can still see it as if it all happened yesterday. The resort was a beautiful property with a sparkling raised pool with views of Jamaica's western cliffs at the rocky coastline near Negril's lighthouse. Rock Cliff's rolling grounds were immaculately kept and we felt like we were in Eden. Lorna and the four children, my youngest sister Cassandra, my nieces Marcia, Desrene, Tracey, and I checked in on a Thursday and began to have one of the best vacations ever. We simply had good family fun in the pool and at the beach. At mealtime, we chatted way up into the night. On the Friday morning, we had breakfast then just lazed around, wondering what to do next.

I remember that day as a cool and clear one. The sea was calm and there was hardly any wind. We spent all day at the beach, away from the hotel, then returned at about three or four in the afternoon. We washed off the white sand, then showered in time to see the spectacular Negril sunset, rated by many as the most magical anywhere in the world.

We were just preparing to have a private dinner later that night when someone from the hotel office came to my room.

"You have a very important call from New York," she said. My mind raced, wondering who would have gone to the trouble to call me all the way in Negril. I got to the office and picked up the line. It was Jackie.

"Lowell, you won't believe what just happened!!" she screamed. There was fear in the next voice too, something I hadn't associated with an ex–undercover cop.

"Your patty supply just got cut off," Boss said in a hurry.

"No . . . Boss!" I shouted into the phone. "I can't believe they did this—why?"

"He never said why." Boss was more composed now. He'd already given me the worst of the news. "All he did was promise me a hundred cases of fifty patties. He said he'll deliver them tomorrow, and then that's it."

My future now rested on the supply of 5,000 beef patties, the main draw for my customers. There seemed to be no room for maneuver and I could not think of an alternative.

"I spoke to the other managers over there," he continued. "They say their boss has made his decision and it's out of their hands . . . Believe me, there's nothing better to expect from that end."

"Boss, call me back," was all I could say. I just couldn't talk anymore. I was scared, with nowhere to turn. Devastated, I hung up the phone and went back to my room. Everything had gone numb. Desrene, Marcia, Tracey, Lorna, and Cassandra were there waiting nervously.

"You won't believe this," I said, and blurted out all

I'd just heard from Jackie and Boss in New York. As soon as I got their initial reactions, I went out to the balcony and stayed for a good long while, fuming and thinking. The indescribable desolation of the moment could only be matched by those early days in the Bronx when I had just emigrated to New York. Options and anger made a mess of my thinking. *Do I need to go back to New York right now? Who's taking me to the airport? Get the luggage . . .*

But then a calm took hold. Instead of fleeing the hotel, I decided to call Pops. *He'll know what to do. He won't think this is the end.*

"Hello . . . Pops?" I must have sounded like the "LoLo" of ten years before, in some moment of vulnerability. "Major problem in New York," I said, almost brusquely.

"What!?"

"They cut off my supply," I explained, the way a little boy tells a parent he's been beaten up. "They won't sell me any more patties."

The news shook him too. "What you sayin'!?" my father pressed. I could hear him talking to Mama: "May— you don't hear what the bwoy say . . . Patty supply cut off!"

It didn't take Pops long to tell me what to do. I've thought about this quality in my father, and I guess he shaped it through a combination of circumstance and responsibility. You don't get to be the father of umpteen children, run a busy company, lead a church, and everything else if you can't be decisive.

"Don't leave," he said calmly.

It was what I needed, that familiar grounding that I didn't always have as things spiraled upward and outward in my life.

"Don't worry about it," he went on. "Some things work together for good for those that love the Lord."

"I don't understand what you're saying . . . What do you mean?" I asked. In that moment, I felt like an unbeliever at the feet of the Prophet.

"All things will work out for you."

His calmness washed over me and I began to think clearly again. *All the operational people are in New York. They won't just throw their hands in the air. At least we have some supply to cover us for the next several days. If I'm a nervous wreck, then I'm no use to the team or to Golden Krust. I need to think.*

And so, despite everything that was going on in New York—the threat to our dreams, the frayed nerves—we stayed in Jamaica for ten days in all, instead of fleeing toward the disaster.

We checked out of Rock Cliff and went to stay at the Fern Hill Hotel in Portland, all the way at the eastern end of the island. My sister Novelet had recommended it, and so we stayed there for three days. It was beautiful—we frolicked about, swam in the pool, and recharged our resolve. We were Hawthornes and we were going to keep our heads above the water.

Not knowing Boss had called before, my sister Jacqueline Robinson telephoned to ask one of the questions I'd been avoiding. "We have no machines," she said. "How are we going to make patties?"

The last official wholesale delivery of patties was made to Golden Krust on the following Monday. Jackie called me again in that all-business way of hers, like someone reading a telegram: "LoLo . . . patties delivered . . . the last one hundred cases." She had been functioning as general manager, directing the efforts of my brothers Milton and Lloyd, my sister "Mother," Boss, and my sister-in-law Velma to keep everything going.

The hundred cases lasted all of seven days. The following week, the team decided to use private cars to canvas the supplier's outlets and purchase more patties. As if acting out a caper-movie plot, they used several cars to pull it off. One person would drive south to Finger Lickin' Bakery on White Plains Road; someone else would go to the downtown food wholesalers Siegmund Strauss, located at Hunts Point Market.

Jackie did a lot of the actual cloak-and-dagger work, using disguises and several different cars to make the purchases. Buying too much from a single spot or using any kind of van would signal that we were taking major commercial quantities, and so we functioned like a special-forces team going to battle in midsized cars.

It is important to point out that a regular sedan can hold fifteen to twenty cases of patties at best, which is only a maximum of 1,000 units. The effort took several people in many raids over many weeks, fanning out to the places where patties were sold wholesale, and then making the rendezvous back at Gun Hill. If my supplier was aware of the strategy, he never let on. What was very clear was that our sudden rise in the business must have been a cause for concern. We had to be stopped. That fact had made things tough, but we were survivors, and there were lots of us with the same last name and the same fire in the belly. We knew we weren't going out of business just yet.

Now, we just had to buckle down and figure out how to make a good commercial Jamaican patty.

It wasn't that we weren't trying. Once again, Lloyd and Velma (plus my cousin Garnett, who was also instrumental in the patty development process) stepped into the breach to begin experimenting with patty meat and crust. Some batches were almost nice, but they were something that people might eat politely and not try again.

For a few days, my siblings actually sold the patties from the wholesalers and the new Golden Krust experimentals at the same time. Some customers asked why we were offering two kinds, which to them was a first in the annals of the product. If you sold a good beef patty, you didn't sell another beside it.

Simply put, our new ones just weren't cutting it. But we were going to have to stop buying finished patties soon enough, and so we simply had to figure it all out. Lloyd and Milton made a horseshoe-shaped pastry stamp to simplify the cutting of crust blanks from the dough. Everyone got down to the business of making prototypes. Because there was no money to buy new machines, six additional staff were hired to cut out patties at a rate of 1,800 per day and keep that part of the operation going around the clock in order to satisfy the market.

Finally, I returned on a late Air Jamaica flight from Kingston. The next day, I was at the manufacturing facility at six a.m. I'd had no sleep. Despite the problems, I found my sister and brother making patties in earnest and generally keeping things together. I pitched in and used Boss's private car to join the undercover operation, hoping I wouldn't be recognized while buying wholesale. I gave Jackie and Lloyd a lot of credit for their decisiveness and problem solving during this time. But I wasn't satisfied with the end product we were putting out. My mind started swirling again. *Can't we buy our own patty machine? Do we have enough money to do this?*

As if sent from above, our pepper supplier, Don Harper, helped us get a line of credit from Barclays Bank. Within two weeks, the bank had miraculously approved a loan of

$70,000 for acquisition of a turnover-making machine. We promptly placed an order in Chicago for a mechanical process called a Colborne pie line. This bought a glimmer of hope.

We still weren't satisfied with the recipe we were using. Despite our best efforts, the patty crust wasn't flaking. Worst of all, the product wasn't holding up in the warmer; the skin was bursting and leaking. Nobody would want a Jamaican patty with the meat dripping out through the crust.

Around this time, I had begun to do a lot of research on the countries that produce pies in large quantities and with good quality. It dawned on me that the English were not just known for fish and chips but also made a traditional kidney pie, which they turned out in great numbers. I figured that this would be good place to start in our quest to develop a good crust for our patties. After weeks of painstaking research, I discovered a company in Cheshire named Burgess Food Machinery. They were known for producing heavy-duty pie lines specially built to handle large-scale production with the quality and consistency we wanted. At a quickly convened meeting with the family team and other shareholders, I announced that I would be heading to London in search of this machine and to also tour several pie manufacturing companies to learn more about formulation and different methods used to produce pie crust.

There was no better person to take along than my brother Raymond, who has a great eye and ear for detail and knows how to stick to a task. We spent hours coming up with a good itinerary and making all the necessary contacts in the UK. A few days later, we got our tickets and set out via British Airways to London Heathrow Airport. Of course, Raymond and I shared a room to take some of the sting out of the cost of accommodation at the Westminster Hotel. Jetlagged but anxious on that first day, we willed ourselves to remain focused on the fact-finding mission. For breakfast, we couldn't resist trying this kidney pie we had talked and read so much about. The meat filling was nothing close to what we were doing in the States at GK. I rather disliked it. The flaky crust, on the other hand, was an epiphany, and we knew this would be a home run if we could get our patty crust to be anything like it.

The next day, Raymond and I caught a train for the two-hour ride to Manchester before switching lines on our way to Cheshire. As the train took us through changing terrain and suburban communities, I couldn't help thinking we were still a far way from solving the puzzle of producing the world's best Jamaican patties. A contact picked us up at the train station, and then took us to the plant where the specialized baking machines were being built.

Coming from the United States and having some idea of manufacturing, we were not very impressed with the factory. The owners had very few finished rigs to show us and what I did see I considered to be works in progress. We were reluctant to give Paul, the owner of the company, the 50 percent down payment required based on my assessment of the operation; after a while, we asked to be shown around to a few factories so we could see some of their machines at work. I also wanted to speak to some of the managers who had bought and were using Burgess machines.

Upon arrival at the Hugh factory, Raymond's eyes were wide with wonder, filled with the scale of production he saw there. I was impressed by the fact that I was instructed to sanitize my shoes before entering the plant, where they were producing a half-million pies a day using several of the type of machine I had come to England to acquire. Based on what I saw, my confidence grew, validating my original feeling that Burgess could make the equipment I needed so desperately.

Raymond and I were pleased, not only because we had found the right solution, but we were also given some in-depth lessons from one of the plant foremen about the different types of Scottish methods for making the best pies. We were so taken with this development that when we were ready to return to the States, we not only paid 50 percent down on a machine for Golden Krust, but also arranged for a top foreman to come to the U.S. to teach us how to make a good kidney pie crust—assuming all along that if he could make good crust for meat pies, he was certain to know how to make one for a beef patty.

Though the man had never visited the United States, he certainly had heard a lot about "Fort Apache," the name given to a tough section of the South Bronx by police in the 41st Precinct. Completely undiscouraged, he was ready to take on the challenges when he arrived within a few weeks of our return. Right away, he began to disseminate a wealth of knowledge to the team that eagerly awaited him, marking another major milestone on our journey to produce a top English crust with our authentic Jamaican twist. The training quickly took hold among our bakers and before long, we had our crust.

Key people like Garnett "Byron" Morrison facilitated the aspect of the bakery that allowed the British training to take hold and make the integration of the new crust formulation and process successful. This is a good place to elaborate on the relationship between the Hawthornes and the Morrisons. For as long as I can remember, our families have been inseparable. The children from each family provided playmates for the other, their ages and number roughly matched ours, and we were always together.

We were also related. Garnett, the director of plant operations (manufacturing), is also my cousin, his mother being my father's sister. As youngsters, we pretended we were preachers, imitating the ones we heard growing up.

Garnett was always quiet and unassuming and I was hardly surprised when he became a minister in addition to being a master baker. He attended Paisley All-Age School and he fetched water in zinc pans before school just as I did. After school, he worked in the bakery and later became the top salesman for Hawthorne & Sons. Garnett emigrated to the United States in 1980, making use of an opportunity to study electrical engineering and digital electronics at several technical institutes. He worked at Granada TV U.S.A. and achieved an amazing command of the technology and other skills, which he brought with him when he accepted our invitation to return to the bakery business. Our gain was high-tech's loss when he joined Golden Krust in New York.

Garnett has overall bakery supervisory responsibility and is a man I trust completely, to the point where if he's in the plant, I never ask how things are going. He was there when we lost our patty supply and is probably the most consistent team member we've ever had. His brother, Burnett Morrison, supervises bread making, and Stelvin "Bragga" Morrison runs the maintenance department. These are three of the most powerful men in the organization, but they are so unassuming that it would be difficult for the casual onlooker to discern.

Having tackled the challenges posed by the crust, our

problems were far from over. Now we had to get the meat right, which is not something you just casually figure out by experimenting with your most expensive component. For example, we were using too much black pepper, and our proportions of meat to the other filler ingredients left something to be desired. The filler we made caused our test efforts to waver somewhere between doughy and soupy. Finally, we admitted defeat, accepting the chilling fact that Hawthorne determination and togetherness couldn't do everything.

An acquaintance with some culinary skills, a man they called "Skin-Up," soon gave us a meat patty formula. To be fair, it was better than the one we were using, but it still wasn't up to snuff. If Golden Krust was going to be a successful baked-goods company, this product we wanted to sell so badly had to be the best. I personally wanted to be the best. And so having found our "golden krust," I still had to find that perfect patty meat as well. Not knowing where to start, it seemed like the quest for the Holy Grail would have been easier.

It was time to find ourselves a chef who held "the secret."

Someone eventually told me about a patty meat chef, an old-timer named Mel, who had worked both in Jamaica and the States and who had gone into semiretirement in Jamaica. Within a month of my trip to the UK, I was on my way back to Jamaica, to Lorna's part of the country, in fact, in search of a man from Maidstone, Manchester. I had no address to go on, no next of kin or friend's address, no listing of any kind that I could use to find him. Just Maidstone.

Traditionally, the roads along Jamaica's south coast,

less traveled than those of the commercial centers and tourist meccas, are not of the best quality. Maidstone lived up to that tradition. It reminded me of Border in a way, somewhat remote, only not as hilly. Whatever could pass as a road was rocky, and where land was not cleared for cultivation or the odd house, all one encountered was brush. It made the going tedious, particularly where there were just no clues to follow. Lorna told me there were no regular bus stops in her village, except for the one in the little main square, where there was a little country shop and a little club.

I found that folks aren't always forthcoming with names and addresses of people they barely know, just to help someone they don't know at all. I felt a sudden rush of panic when I thought that nobody around may know him by his given name, which was the only name I had for my quest. I didn't even have much of a useful description.

The man could have walked right by me—and out of my grand scheme—without my recognizing him. "Do you know a gentleman named Mel?" I'd ask, suppressing my frustration with as much country manners as I could muster.

"No," the folks would reply with a bemused kind of sympathy. My desperation must have showed as I made four to five stops like that, without luck.

Then, there was a change in fortune. I noticed an old bearded man nearby, wearing khaki and a pair of black rubber boots. He was leading a donkey, carrying yams that hung heavily over both sides of the animal.

"You want Mel?" he inquired without my asking. He'd caught wind of my feverish inquiries. "Him live up the hill, past the school, and . . ."

I forgot the exact text of what he told me, but I was familiar enough with the way people give directions in rural Jamaica: perfectly accurate to the person giving them, but to the uninitiated, they could be utterly useless. At least I had something to go on.

Stopping at another shop, I asked a young man where I could find Mel. He gave me more directions, but I was starting to think the man didn't actually exist. Feeling like I was running out of options, I walked up to an older man, a gentle-looking fellow in his late fifties. He was short, dark-skinned, and very polite.

"Do you know Mr. Mel?" I asked the man. "Can you help me find him?"

"Ah me name so," he said.

"You're Mel?" I fought back my excitement, already in negotiation mode. "I've been looking for you."

We had a good little chat before I said, "I hear you're a great cook. I need you to come to the U.S. to help me."

"A wha' you a say?" he asked, as if I was crazy.

"Do you have a passport?"

"No sah, mi no have no passport . . ."

I felt the devastation coming. The wait for a Jamaican passport in those days could be anywhere from several days to several months. I wasn't going to have months.

"But mi can get one in record time," he assured me.

"How soon can you travel?" I asked him, grinning widely. He said he was doing some farming and building a shop, but he'd postpone all that and come to the U.S.

"Mi have some things fi clear up," he replied, "then mi can come."

The man was in New York within a month, in the fall of 1992.

Instinctively, I didn't rush Mel into cooking a 200-pound batch of meat right away. For an operation like ours, that amount of production costs a small fortune. Once we started to prep for his first test batch, though, I realized that something was wrong. The man seemed a bit uncomfortable and hesitant for an experienced chef with the "secret." For one thing, he didn't write down his ingredient list for the meat recipe.

As it turned out, Mel could neither read nor write. What was even more tragic was that once he got going, the first sample he cooked really didn't taste all that great. *Is this what all that effort was for? Our recipes don't work the way we want, and we can't get by just selling breads, buns, and bullas. And we can't go back to buying finished patties . . .*

I called for my brother Lloyd and sister-in-law Velma and got their opinions on the flavor. They concurred. The meat wasn't anything special. For that moment, I was up against it again. The family and everyone else would ask why we went to all this trouble, just to cook meat that tasted no better than the well-intentioned stuff we were already doing. But we refused to believe that his reputation was a myth. The mediocre flavor could mean only one thing: old Mel was hiding something.

We asked him to revise his efforts and discreetly gave him some room to operate. Allowing him more personal space and privacy must have worked because sure enough, the next tasting was an utter revelation.

Since the very early days, I've had a habit of touching food in the plant with a naked sterilized hand. So I put my finger into the kettle—which was going along at 160 degrees—and sampled the meat. It was unbelievable. All the memories of fresh patties back home came flooding back. Not only was this flavor authentic—it had to be the best I'd ever tasted up to that point. Now we could swing for the fences. We had our real Jamaican patty ready.

I never even stopped to consider doing a consumer test. We stuffed Mel's creation into some crust as fast and in as much quantity as we could, baked the batches, and immediately put them out to our hungry customers. We couldn't bake enough of them during that time.

The big new pastry machine we had ordered was already on its way. My confidence level grew by leaps and bounds as the organization demonstrated its capacity to handle all challenges. Customers were coming to Gun Hill Road in droves as the word spread about the new Golden Krust patty. This was a very enjoyable and hectic time, when we could all watch our brand growing right before our eyes, gaining momentum almost entirely by word of mouth.

Even as we celebrated, we were mindful of the all-important lessons we had learned about thinking clearly in a crisis and keeping ourselves open to opportunity. We were going to make sure we seized this one with both hands.

CHAPTER ELEVEN
Dough Rising

By December of 1992, sales topped two million dollars for the first time. We were all convinced that a period of unprecedented growth and expansion lay ahead. But it wasn't always smooth sailing. Every mile of the journey had twists and turns; in the end it was our resourcefulness, creativity, and fixity of purpose that brought us through.

The Colborne machinery arrived, and I recognized immediately that it wouldn't fit in the existing configuration of the building. Fortunately, at this time my brother Milton was living in the two-bedroom apartment above the bakery, and allowed us to use his apartment's kitchen to install a forty-gallon kettle for cooking patty meat. The installation of this piece of equipment made the critical difference to the production process. But not even a family member can be reasonably asked to live indefinitely with the powerful patty meat aroma seeping into all his clothes and belongings. Predictably, the operation hastened his departure from the upstairs flat, leaving the building exclusively to the production of Golden Krust products.

Having taken over the entire apartment, our next task was to make some necessary renovations. It was at this time that I called the landlord and offered to finalize the purchase of his building. Back then, most commercial banks did not see us as a viable entity, and we would certainly have had difficulty raising money to buy the place, regardless of price. It wasn't so much that the banks wouldn't lend to small businesses; they did. The reluctance was due to the fact that most small so-called "Jamaican" businesses were not perceived as enterprises that could consistently generate the revenue required to repay a bank loan. For the most part, they were seen as little places that fed the stereotype, hawking herbal juice and reggae music, or as fronts for selling drugs.

By the spring of 1993, we had become independent of all other patty manufacturers for good. The thirteen locations already established were either outright Golden Krust locations or agents of the company's products. Demand was spiralling upward and the 800 square feet of work space in the basement at Gun Hill Road was woefully inadequate.

Golden Kust had reached a critical crossroads. With tremendous demand for our products and thousands of customers to satisfy daily, something had to be done to get capacity on par with demand.

We recognized that since we now owned the building at Gun Hill Road, we could move forward with the expansion of our flagship location. We knew we had available space at the back of the building, but we were also aware that we'd be taking a huge risk, since we were planning a $300,000 expansion on a site that could not accommodate a USDA facility either in scope or size. But we had no choice. Demand for our baked goods was literally growing by the hour and we couldn't make them on the sidewalk.

I contacted Mount Vernon top architect Errol McIntosh to lay out a plan that could facilitate the production of Jamaican patties and also serve as a manufacturing plant for bread, cakes, and buns. This was a tall order, but in light of Errol's experience as a former commissioner of buildings, we were certain that he could navigate his way through the city codes and get us an approved permit to construct a 4,000-square-foot headquarters for Golden Krust on Gun Hill Road.

Without a doubt, Errol felt pressured by our demands for the largest possible facility that would fit on the property. That was only half of it. We were also pushing him to be finished with an approved plan in two weeks.

Errol met with us, presented the first draft with all the restrictions and variations, and in less than an hour we gave the plans our blessing. There were certain details and requirements that in other circumstances we could have contested, but time was of the essence. We didn't have the luxury to sit around or to fight City Hall because we were pushing to finish the expansion and seize the moment.

I recall McIntosh telling us that for this plan to be approved, he would have to build a 10,000-gallon underground water retention tank to prevent the sewer from overflowing and putting excess demands on the city's sewer system. I knew in my heart that I could have sent him back to find a way to work around it; instead, we gave him the green light to build the tank and make it part of the plan to prevent running water from entering municipal sewer lines.

Once the plan satisfied city requirements, we met with Nima Badaly from Badaly & Badaly Architects. I figured that when you want to build at the speed that we needed, their combination of skill sets was perfect and necessary to keep us humming. Finally, in the spring of 1993, a contract was executed between Badaly and Golden Krust. The agreement's clauses carried stiff financial penalties if the contractor failed to perform or complete building the facility in the time specified.

To execute the work plan as smoothly as possible, we had to continue to produce in the basement to keep up with product demand, and also keep our supplies of water and electricity intact while all this was going on.

On the first scheduled work day, Badaly's team arrived bright and early with all their subcontractors and heavy equipment in tow. *These guys really look like they can do the job!* I thought. I was pleased when the builder introduced his crew, which included four brothers from Belize: Sedrick, Alwin, Alvin, and The Dread. The brothers and the others worked miracles, getting the job done in under six weeks.

We had mixed feelings, however, about the completion of the new space at Gun Hill, and even during construction we were already getting the surprise of our lives. By now, we were operating in Connecticut and New Jersey, as well as doing small distribution of beef patties for wholesale. Even as the first block was being laid, it was clear from our order numbers and the crowds in the stores that we had already outgrown our unbuilt facility. But there was no slowing down. We just had to finish the project anyway and cross the next bridge when we got there. I was anxious, but I didn't wait around for the last building block to be installed. I was busy scouting for an opportunity to build the next facility.

Under federal law, no business can manufacture or distribute poultry and beef products without a United States Department of Agriculture (USDA) license. We had come too far to be operating outside the law, so that created an even greater sense of urgency. GK couldn't operate any longer like bakers who occasionally popped some meat into a crescent-shaped pie crust. If Golden Krust was going to sell in quantity to other businesses and across state lines, the operation would have to be run entirely by the book.

This was a period when so many profound things were happening to me: my family was adjusting to life in Westchester; we were undergoing rapid, internally funded expansion, which sapped up cash flow; there were issues with partnerships and the headaches of grappling with tri-state regulations; we were still working to perfect GK patties even as we fought a battle with the Mafia; in general, we did our best to manage the complexities of an expanding family business.

I was enormously grateful then that no matter the circumstances, I had my mother, who was able to laugh with me. Man, my mama loved to laugh. Most importantly, I had Christ the Anchor and the One who enabled me to do all things despite the challenges. I wholeheartedly believed then, as now, that where there are constraints and challenges, boundless opportunities often lie.

We bought two hundred-gallon kettles to increase capacity and keep up with ever-rising demand. Sensing that we were on the verge of something truly big and sustainable. In our haste to expand, we made the mistake of buying a commercial oven for Gun Hill, which turned out to be too tall to fit into the available space. Our predicament was made worse by the fact that the oven could not be returned. Nor did we have enough time to sell it and acquire a smaller one. So once again, the Hawthornes put their creative minds together and came up with a solution. We dropped the floor to the required level and created additional space for the equipment to fit.

I'd always heard the term "hand over fist" to describe an operation that turns over goods so fast that everything becomes a blur. This is an apt description of the Golden Krust operation in those early years when the brand was gaining serious momentum. We literally could not bake patties fast enough, and at one point were putting out product around the clock, baking bread at night and patties all day. Unable to expand capacity in the space we had added to the first retail location at Gun Hill Road, we knew it was time to find ourselves a stand-alone factory. We quickly identified a property at 2242 Light Street off Dyre Avenue, since it was in our general neighborhood, then engaged Errol McIntosh to design the new manufacturing facility. He was aware that time was of the essence, and we were already visualizing the complete project. About the time McIntosh's drawings were complete, reality caught up to the speed of our progress.

Concerned about the feasibility of our plan, I met with the management team, and everyone agreed that the Light Street location wouldn't work. The new factory we were about to build promised to be immediately obsolete, too small to accommodate our projected capacity upon completion.

A chance encounter took us to a real estate broker in Mount Vernon, New York, who happened to have a line on a property in the Bronx. It had roughly the space we needed. Once we got the full details, I discovered that this prospect was even better than it first appeared: Irving Feinberg's building on Park Avenue in the South Bronx once produced hot dogs. What's more, the factory already had USDA approval.

In June 1993, we acquired the building on Park Avenue and rented Feinberg's next-door property for storage. Once again, we called in Nima Badaly and set them to work to finish our build-out in three months. The builders promised they could deliver.

In its previous configuration, the facility had been set

up for meat cutting and processing. It already had a good freezer, drainage, and floor, which meant that there would be less to build and install for our purposes. My brothers Milton and Lloyd did most of the demolition work, while I made several trips with plans in hand to Washington, D.C., to ensure that our plant design, product formulation, and workflow would meet USDA specifications. If all went well, we would make November of 1993 the target for the launch of our federal manufacturing plant.

Making food products, especially those containing meat, is serious business in the United States, requiring approvals from the Animal and Plant Health Inspection Service (APHIS), the Food Safety Inspection Service (FSIS), Grain Inspection Packers and Stockyards Administration (GIPSA), Federal Grain Inspection Service (FGIS), and Agricultural Marketing Service (AMS). There are also U.S. Customs Service requirements to satisfy to avoid detention of imported product components.

The prospect of moving our operations to the next level excited us and kept everyone's energy level high, but the process was tedious, filled with big and small details that constantly required our attention. For example, all our packaging would now have to display the legend *USDA Approved*, along with our federal ID number, once final inspection had been completed. In anticipation of our approval, we confidently went ahead as planned with our grand opening at Park Avenue on a Saturday, with USDA inspection scheduled for the following Monday. We were ready to become only the third federally approved patty manufacturer in the United States at that time.

The celebration received a large turnout. Mama and Pops were on hand, as were Lorna and her parents, a host of other relatives and friends, my business partners (who happened to be my siblings), Kai Ng, and several dignitaries from local government, to cut the ribbon with me. The good wishes and optimism were palpable as everyone swapped congratulations and milled about. If we had stopped to think about it at the time, we would have been amazed to recall that just eight months before, we were still buying and reselling someone else's patties!

On the big day, Monday, we certainly looked ready. The plant's walls and floors had been cleaned, stainless steel surfaces gleamed, and everyone on hand was dressed in white smocks and jackets, ready for our close-up. Two field inspectors and a supervisor arrived and quietly set about checking the equipment and surfaces.

Their assessment was short and sour.

"You're not ready," one of the inspectors told me. It turned out that some of the stainless steel had smudges, and it was clear that our idea of clean, in general, was not the same as theirs. We knew we'd have to redouble our efforts and get everything shipshape for another inspection, and I had no doubt that initial inspections for the federal licensing have a high failure rate.

The reality was that we had worked nonstop in a tight time frame; now we would have to shut down for a few days, perfect everything, and get the approval then. There was one problem with all that: we were unable to produce any patties for three days, because the new machinery for the product was at the new location, with Gun Hill—which was by this time only producing bread and other baked goods—waiting to be fed.

Our reinspection went off problem-free, and by Thursday of the same week, Golden Krust produced its first patty under federal license. We were now qualified for nationwide supply. The transition had been difficult, because some of our related functions were split between the two plants. Since our main office was at Gun Hill Road, the workday began in the South Bronx at the new location and ended at Gun Hill.

Armed with our new and prestigious designation, we immediately embarked on a new growth spurt, targeting schools, prisons, and supermarkets. By 1994, in less than a year, Golden Krust was selling patties to the prison system; in 1995, we acquired the building we rented adjoining the Park Avenue plant and started exploring opportunities to purchase other adjoining buildings. Around this time, we were able to get $1.4 million in loans from the Small Business Administration and HSBC to carry out the expansion.

HSBC would later appoint me to a board in recognition of my business skills and local connections, which allowed them to tap into resources they could in turn bring to the banking sector. Far more than the honor that it was, the appointment served to give me great insight into the inner workings of large banks, showing me what they look for when deciding to partner with a business. Later, all this experience would come in handy when it was time to help hundreds of franchisees get established in the U.S. with financing.

Mel, our man from Maidstone in Jamaica, continued to amaze us with the consistency and quality of his cooking. People ate the patties as if they were addicted to them, and both production and sales figures climbed steadily. My chef was not a young man, however, and with Golden Krust's increasing responsibility to several families, employees, and the bank, we had to be sure that our formula was standardized and protected. Technically, since Mel never told me how he cooked the meat, I still didn't actually know how to make my own patty. And after all the time he had been with us, he didn't offer to document the recipe.

As he did when he had just arrived, Mel always made a verbal request for each new batch of his specific ingredients. At best, I knew for sure what items were in the filling, but how could I figure out the quantities for a recipe that was never written down? The ingredients were all fairly basic items, which made the elusive recipe all the more frustrating, hiding in plain sight. We couldn't just dismiss Mel for being secretive, nor could we force him to reveal his proportions.

I resolved to unravel the puzzle by focusing on the creation of my own blend, first by using my best guess at what proportions were put into our kettles, with the help of Velma, Lloyd, and the taste buds of the rest of the family. Slowly but surely, Lloyd's blend of meat, thyme, scallions, herbs, and other items began to taste the way Mel's did, first in small batches, then in larger ones. Then, I adjusted for quantities of basic ingredients and spices until today's Golden Krust beef patty standard was born. I became the holder of my own secret.

Old Mel eventually returned to his shop, crops, and retirement in Jamaica, and died around 1999 from an asthma attack. Mel died without fully revealing the recipe we had hired him to develop. One of the chefs he had brought in called to give me the news. Saddened and worried for his family, I flew to Jamaica soon after to help with arrangements for his memorial service. The whole GK family was devastated. At the time, Mel was the first Golden Krust employee to pass on. He had come to us at a time when we were finding our feet, and I'll never forget how willing he was to drop everything he was doing at the time to join us.

I've made sure to keep in touch with his wife over the years and I see to her material needs from time to time.

By 1996, the year we added public schools as a major client source, we bought two other next-door buildings. One, a garage, was perfect for siting our maintenance operation. The following year, we added another building on the block that had been in the lumber trade. That location became our headquarters. Another spot, a former plumber's, became the new location for the remaining bakery operation from Gun Hill Road. Within ten years, we had gutted our original manufacturing space to install state-of-the-art pie lines and other equipment that brought our operation up to the highest available level of technology. This was accomplished with significant support from Bank of America.

Today, Golden Krust has space in excess of 100,000 square feet at Park Avenue—and we're seeking more space in the area. To keep pace with ten dozen GK locations from Connecticut to Florida, the company also established minibakeries in Orlando, Miami, and Atlanta to keep fresh supply in the South, allowing the Park Avenue plant to produce patties and jerk chicken for all the points in the system, which today includes schools, prisons, supermarkets, and shopping clubs.

After our strongest period of steady growth and expansion, sometime in 1995, we were convinced of the Golden Krust magic and decided to allow family, friends, and customers—who were constantly asking for an opportunity—to become a part of the Golden Krust success story. Franchising the brand seemed the way to go.

The family met shortly thereafter and gave serious consideration to the idea of taking the organization in this direction. The founding directors also met with our other siblings who, for one reason or another, were not at that time part of the business. They were offered a small equity stake. Those family members willing to participate and invest in the Golden Krust concept effectively expanded the ownership of the corporation as it prepared to become a franchise organization.

Though it was a daunting step, we next decided to find a knowledgable attorney to guide us through the procedures and pitfalls of franchising, but there were few listed in the Yellow Pages. Since there were clearly not many franchise lawyers around—and certainly no black ones, as far as we could determine—we proceeded on our own, doing the basic research on franchise law in bookstores and libraries. At the time, there were only three black-owned franchise businesses in the U.S., and not one was a household name.

From those listed we chose franchise attorney Vincent DeBiase, who was from Corbally, Gartland and Rappleyea, a suburban firm of about thirty lawyers. Their fees were lower than the $500 an hour we'd have to pay a lawyer in the city. Lorraine, Jackie, our CPA Alfred Simms, and I took the hundred-mile drive north to Poughkeeepsie, a small town in upstate New York, to see DeBiase for a discussion on franchising. There we struck gold. The firm was small enough to charge $175 an hour. More importantly, they were franchising experts, and they were also big enough to represent GK in many areas of the law.

Our conversation, which by itself was worth the trip, went something like this:

"Are you sure you want to go into this business?"

"Yes," I replied. "That's what we're here to discuss."

"You're gonna get sued by franchisees," he warned. "If you don't wanna get sued, don't do it . . ." Finally he said,

"I'll tour your stores and factory," as if he already knew that we were on a fool's errand, doomed to fail.

He went on a tour of the plant with us anyway. Sure enough, he was ready with comments after reviewing the locations in our small network.

"You're not ready for franchising," DeBiase said matter-of-factly. It was this kind of honesty and expertise that would later land him a seat on the Golden Krust board.

"What do you mean?" I asked, deflated.

"You'll have to knock them down and start over. The locations must all look the same. Moreover, you'll need manuals, training centers, good staff, consistency, and proper systems in place."

Undaunted, we went from store to store, redesigning them all to achieve uniformity. The visual concept was a simple purple and white design with red and yellow accents. But it wasn't created by an interior designer. A graphic artist created the whole thing.

Everything had to be redone. By early 1996, we finished the conversions satisfactorily and started doing the application paperwork. We hired a California company, Writer's Block, to create our operational manual, franchise manual, and our marketing and human resource manual. Alfred Simms did the financial statement required to start the franchising process. I used a lot of the time spent in the air to redraft and rewrite the manuals until they satisfied the required standards. After months of research, SWOT analysis, and assessments, we took the calculated risk and applied for the franchise license.

Information about the impending franchising of Golden Krust spread like wildfire, and people seemed to come from every direction seeking details on how to get in on the action. On May 23, 1996, we were granted our franchise license. At the time, this was the greatest moment in the history of Golden Krust. We had never celebrated any milestone the way we did that day.

Immediately, a franchisee was waiting to set up the first independent Golden Krust restaurant. Earl Chin, an accountant at a Brooklyn welding company, went about building his store to get an early start as the first full-fledged location not owned by the company or its partners.

He couldn't finish the build-out by himself, however, after his founding partner was killed in a knife attack on a golf course in Pelham, New York. Unwavering in his enthusiasm for the venture and the Golden Krust concept, Earl got his boss' son, David O'Brien, to join him in completing the store and forming a franchising partnership.

In 2009, they would join us in celebrating fourteen years of association with the Golden Krust brand as Franchisee #1.

In less than a decade, we had transformed a small bread- and bun-making operation into one of the fastest-growing Caribbean enterprises in America. Finally, after years of trepidation, anxiety, and fear, the company had arrived at a major crossroads and was poised for great things to come.

I am not a big fan of family favoritism per se, but it is certainly a characteristic of any family-owned business, whether it's the Waltons, Maloofs, or Hawthornes. As leader of one of America's foremost black-owned Caribbean family businesses, I had to create the type of environment where everyone who works for the organization feels that s/he belongs to the whole entity through recognition, inclusion, and reward. It's true that family may have an advantage in getting hired, but learning the business at all levels, helping to advance the company mission—and just plain working hard to earn your paycheck—are all mandatory at Golden Krust, regardless of one's last name. Believe it or not, most of the family members who joined the company were suited for their various jobs by what you could call QBE (qualified by experience). The positions they each held, for the most part, were based on their past employment, education, and training received both prior to and since joining the company.

A lot has been written about my family and our success in the venture we started in 1989. The stories generally refer to how my siblings and I pooled resources and talents, maintaining commonality of purpose and keeping costs low. But little has been publicized about the tremendous personal toll the business and its tensions have taken on us, with all the frayed nerves, health issues, and personal challenges my relatives have endured along the way. As I read that extraordinary story about the Hawthornes and Golden Krust, published by the *Sun-Sentinel* in 2009, my thoughts turned to Mama. I wished she could have seen what had been built on the foundations she and the family had laid.

Strong families in business together have the benefit of capitalizing on individual strengths, but should also remain honest about never giving someone a job s/he can't handle. If, for example, your company would never hire someone with no experience or aptitude for office work, then a family member should never be hired and assigned to fill such a role.

Of course, every family has weaknesses in the chain. Ours is no exception. I suppose the frailty shows itself in occasional lapses in discipline, from things as simple as absence at family gatherings to taking shortcuts with important company procedures. Far more serious are those times when a family member is or has become unsuited for a job and has to be either reassigned within the organization—or separated from it altogether.

There's no more uncomfortable feeling than going to work knowing that a sibling's or cousin's job is no longer tenable. It's all the more difficult because the relative has, in all likelihood, already been transferred to departments where s/he can either become more effective—or relatively less destructive. And so when finally it is clear that the individual can neither fit nor function, the professional bond has to be severed.

I don't remember feeling regretful when a Hawthorne had to be fired. If the termination is warranted, it's what needs to be done regardless of blood. What is always difficult is the series of uncomfortable family moments in the months or days afterward. Thankfully, we have not gone through that difficulty very often.

CHAPTER TWELVE
Shaped by Tragedy

During the early years of the business, there were times when I felt sure I was looking at the beginning of the end for Golden Krust. With the benefit of hindsight I can now see that on those occasions, we had either been slow to act or had neglected brand development. At critical stages of our development, we had even offered products to the market that hardly represented the best of our capability. However, in a strong family-oriented enterprise, our collective will, resourcefulness, and pride were enough to take us through.

I didn't know then that none of those setbacks would compare with the agony I would experience when faced with the mortality of loved ones. Whereas I had developed the resilience to cope with economic reversals of any magnitude, I had little confidence that I would be able to cope in the same way with family tragedy. I always felt that it would have a profoundly debilitating effect on me and consequently threaten the very survival of the business. I'm as competitive as the next CEO, but I differ from most in one significant way: I would gladly trade the entire business for the life or the restored health of any family member. On a couple of occasions, I almost did.

The first was in 1994. Mama seemed robust, healthy, and cheerful, keeping up her normal routine of babysitting and being a good grandmother to Lorraine's two children, Tulicia and Latalya, in their home in Yonkers, New York.

One evening, Mama mentioned quite nonchalantly that her stomach was not feeling well. We were not alarmed because we thought it was a case of simple indigestion. But the pain continued for days despite the antacids and home remedies applied. Even so, we took her to the doctor fully expecting her to recuperate quickly.

A few days later we took her to the Montefiore Medical Center for a thorough examination. Then, after weeks of tests, we got the news we were dreading: Mama had the big "C"—cancer—and was termianlly ill. All my siblings, nieces, nephews, and friends held daily vigils at her bedside. Despite our best efforts, Mama died and was buried in her native home of Jamaica.

For a while after she passed on, I stopped answering my mail. As a result, I lost some opportunities for expansion, including potential contracts for 50,000 halal patties a month with the New York State prison system. What kept me going was the conviction that Mama would have wanted us to continue the vision of the family business and to seize every opportunity to ensure its growth and success. That was my motivation as I recovered and took a new hold of the operations which had slipped somewhat in those few months. I found my feet again, and throughout that recovery period, it was as if Mama was there with us, helping to hold it together. A blessing came when we got a prison contract to supply regular patties instead.

A second crisis surfaced in 2001, the same year America would come under devastating attack by terrorists on September 11.

The year began pleasantly enough, with Lorna and I going away for a short vacation. Soon after we returned we came face-to-face with a near-tragedy when the life of my eldest son, Haywood, came under mortal threat.

On the day in question, Lorna was at work at head-quarters, doing what she does best by keeping track of all the employees' time and issues in her capacity as director of human resources. I had just turned forty-one and had been advised by Dr. Hector Estepan to have a colonoscopy. I thought I was too young to have this exam done, but figured, *Who am I to question my doctor?*

Trevor Lawrence, a man who had worked with GK in both construction and maintenance, was one of Golden Krust's early employees. He'd been taken on as a janitor when the enterprise started at Gun Hill Road. He quickly earned promotions through sheer dedication to his work and even moved up to do some baking.

A valued employee, Trevor had built a well-deserved reputation for honesty and integrity. He always took more than a casual interest in security at the plant.

"I try to protect the company," is the way he puts it. He is truly one of the most loyal and trustworthy men I've ever known. As conscientious as Trevor was in the protection of company property, however, he was even more concerned for my personal safety. As a rule, he never left work until I was in my car and on my way home.

Trevor often said that he'd take a bullet for me. Thankfully, our general security procedures are evolving and improving all the time, and so I never anticipated that the day would come when Trevor would attempt to keep that promise.

On that spring day, things were humming along at the Bronx plant as they always did at about one in the afternoon. The morning loads had left the plant and some trucks were already returning with cash and orders from franchise and wholesale deliveries. One of Haywood's responsibilities at this stage of the day was to receive some of the large amounts of cash brought in by the drivers. Unknown to him as he sat in his car near the plant, a hooded man had been lurking around, casing the place and observing the cash transactions.

Unnoticed, the man came up to Haywood's window and demanded money. Haywood did his best to remain calm, and handed him a couple thousand dollars. But before making his escape, the robber fired a shot that ripped into the top of the car's door frame, just over my son's head.

Running and looking behind him, the man fired two more shots as he made his escape. If the guy thought he was about to get away scot-free like a regular grab-and-run thief, he soon found out how mistaken he was. Trevor, despite being unarmed, went after the robber in a dead run, and very quickly closed in on him. The assailant, who must have concluded that Trevor was crazy, fired five more times. Thankfully, Trevor tripped and fell, unhurt. His fall may have saved his life that day.

As the robbery was in progress, I was under the effects of anesthesia, with no clue about what was taking place. It wasn't until very late in the evening that I was told of the near-fatality of my son, who has grown up to become a very responsible businessman. At six foot three and very solidly built, he is often mistaken for one of my brothers. Some ask him which football teams he played for. Anyone who succeeds him at work will have big shoes to fill—literally.

As it turned out, Haywood's encounter with a gunman was but a foretaste of what was to come three summers later.

Living outside the Caribbean, I longed to create an atmosphere with the power to transport me to the islands. I love water and the tropical ambiance so much that having a running stream was one of my strict requirements when I sought a property on which to build my dream home. Lorna didn't care much for water, and not being a swimmer, she had no interest in a stream whatsoever. In all our years of marriage, I haven't flown too often on one wing, but this time I had to. So in 2000, I found the place to realize my dream in a small Westchester town, water and all.

The property we selected was in northeast Westchester County, less than a mile from our home on Route 100A. The beautiful green area, which is home to about 7,000 families, had the brook, the space, and the other location factors that we insisted upon. Other than the water and all the other beauty that came with the property, the locale we had chosen had a very progressive school system, which allowed us to choose from three public high schools for our children—Pleasantville, Briarcliff, and Sleepy Hollow. This was new for us, as not many communities present such flexibility in school choice. We seized the opportunity, deciding to register our children at Pocantico Hills Central Elementary in Sleepy Hollow and Briarcliff High.

Our home at the time was only 1,700 square feet and because we were planning to build a much larger one, our limited experience gave us no idea of what features and details a new place of this size should have. We even subscribed to *Architectural Digest* and several other magazines for inspiration.

Giving in to our curiosity and sense of adventure, we decided to pose as homebuyers and get appointments to view houses that were on the market. Mostly, we focused on upscale areas such as Stony Point, Bedford, Armonk, and several neighborhoods in Westchester.

We made sure that we dressed the part, drove our best car, and spoke with authority. I remember that at one point, we wanted to see the inside of an Armonk house so badly that we took our attorney Michael Aspinal with us to ensure that we were treated as serious buyers. Only a serious buyer, I figured, would bring his lawyer on such a trip.

After days and months of collecting information and discussion about the concept, the family had done enough research and decided on the final design. I was so impressed with the fantastic work they had done with our manufacturing facilities that I entrusted Nima Badaly with the responsibility of building our new custom home. Once again, we would set Nima an ambitious schedule. They were required to finish the project within six months.

When it came time for school registration, we had not yet sold our old home or moved into the school district. After speaking to the school principals and explaining the situation, it was agreed that the kids could begin school while our home was being built.

What came next was shocking, heartbreaking, and sobering. A few days after construction began, word got out in our community that blacks were moving in. Early one morning, as we walked from our old home to the building excavation site, we came upon signs spray painted on the bulldozer and the building material accumulated on the site. The graffiti said, *Die niggers die*.

We immediately called the police. The local newspaper and the Westchester cable news channel turned up to cover this case of racial bias. The strangest thing was that this was less than a quarter-mile from where we still lived. I'm not sure if any of my neighbors felt like those racists did, but it was hard for us to shake the fact that for the first time in the twenty years that we had lived in the United States, we were experiencing blatant racism. After all that my family had done to foster race-neutral community relations through business and philanthropic activity, we were the targets of the kind of simple-minded attack we had only previously seen on the news. It made me angry, but didn't dull my enthusiasm for our move in any way.

Lorna cried a great deal that day, but I comforted her. "We've worked too hard for what we've achieved," I said, "to let anyone keep us out of any neighborhood." We continued to build our home and watched with pride as it came out of the ground and took shape. True to my builder's word, it was completed within the six-month time frame. We were grateful and welcoming when police commissioners, town officials, and many politicians came by to show their support.

To heighten the effect of my Caribbean theme, I imported a fake coconut palm from China that had been given to me by one of my contractors. I added trees and plants, exotic koi fish, water wheels, bridges over the brook, and wild birds, all topped off with rock-shaped speakers so I could rock to the beautiful sounds of reggae music. Any illusion I was able to create would disappear by the time Old Man Winter stopped by, but at least I'd found my own Caribbean sanctuary in the backyard. What's more, we had managed to get away from the dangerous roadway that fronted our first Westchester house, which had been home for ten years.

The first month after we moved in, we invited all our neighbors, along with the children's school principals, to have a school board meeting at our residence. We used the occasion to break the ice and try to ease whatever tensions remained. It worked, and we have developed friendships, business opportunities, and a more rewarding sense of community as a result. At the end of the day, all we ever wanted was to live in our new home in peace.

Always with GK in mind, I also seized the opportunity to create new customers by serving some of our famous patties as hors d'oeuvres at the school board meeting that day.

At the time, I did not realize the full impact the incident had on my thirteen-year-old son, Daren. The revelation came in 2009 when he wrote his personal statement to support his application to law school, which included the following:

> Intently watching the television through blurry eyes; my face almost pressed up against the screen. The pile of Kleenex tissues next to me was the last of the box, which ultimately led to my damp sleeves, and I had lost interest in the hot chocolate that sat beside me on the table; a failed attempt at cheering me up. The news reporter asked my mom how she felt about the people who had egged and spray-painted our new home with racial slurs, demanding that we to leave the neighborhood. She responded that it was wrong. We had done nothing to deserve this far-from-warm welcome, and she feared for the safety of her family; a fear that I too was beginning to experience. A firm hand rested on my shaking shoulders as my father, who had just entered the room, said, "It is okay, son; life is not perfect or fair, but you have to be empowered and walk as a man. This will bring you success in the future." Unable to sleep, I stared at the ceiling that whole night fighting back tears. My family had been attacked on the basis of our race and I could not think of anything more unjust. My father's words repeated in my head. Life is not fair. Be empowered. He was right.

After reading it, I could only conclude that a person never knows what a child goes through or how severely affected he or she can be by certain experiences.

* * *

I still get numb thinking about the events of a beautiful and cloudless Saturday night in August 2004. The house had been quieter than usual as my second son Omar had left in his new car to attend a party at his aunt's house in Pleasantville.

I had fallen asleep very soon after going to bed, only to be awakened by the phone. On the other end of the line was my daughter Monique, but I had difficulty recognizing her voice at first. Her words were punctuated by shrill screams and sobbing, which made her incoherent. I finally understood that she was with Stayton, my adopted brother's son, and that they were just about three minutes from our house. Even before I was fully awake, I got the impression that she was hurt, but probably not too badly as she began speaking a little more clearly.

Hurriedly, I got dressed. After driving for a few minutes, I found Monique in a neighbor's yard, crying. She was able to tell me that after the party, she had set out minutes behind Omar in another car on her way home. She stopped when she came upon the familiar gray BMW which had clearly been in an accident. She called me at that moment.

By the time I arrived at the scene, the police and paramedics were already there. Monique, still in shock, just kept screaming, "Omar! Omar! Omar!"

It took me just a few seconds to figure out the crash scenario. Omar was the only driver involved. The car had veered and hit a ditch on the side of the road, flipped over, and rammed into the trunk of a tree. The vehicle was totaled. I would later learn that my son had fallen asleep returning from the family party and run off the road.

Omar was unconscious when I got to him. I completely broke down, but managed to get into the ambulance where paramedics were prepping him for the hospital. I can't remember who told Boss Rhoden about the accident, but he says he "flew from the World Trade Center where [he] was on patrol to Westchester in what felt like ten minutes."

The assessment was more grim than anyone could have imagined. My son had sustained injuries to his head, spine, and ankle. I was told he was bleeding from his brain, and to me, he seemed near death as he lay there all bloody, wearing a neck brace and his head covered in bandages. I went to the hospital every day for ten days, shaking like a leaf on many of those occasions.

Our family profile and the business had become increasingly prominent in local media over the years. As a result, news of the accident spread quickly through informal channels to customers, franchisees, and friends, who were soon making the trip to the hospital in droves. At the same time, New York news outlets ran ominous headlines:

GOLDEN KRUST CEO's SON IN CRITICAL CONDITION
BRIARCLIFF FOOTBALL STAR IN COMA

We would have preferred to deal with this tragedy as privately as possible, but were just unable to avoid the publicity that the accident generated.

My son was lucky. Highly skilled surgeons and nurses took special care of him. Omar would suffer significant short-term memory loss and even had to learn to walk all over again. Praise God, he has made a full recovery. His survival and rehabilitation are testimony to God's unfailing goodness and the sustaining power of faith.

Omar remembers just about nothing of his ordeal, not the falling asleep, the impact, nor those desperate minutes that passed as he was taken from the wreck and brought to the hospital. Throughout this time, I stayed away from the office for weeks, consumed with grief and fear. Family and friends tell me I completely shut down at that time and was pretty useless to the company. I decided that if my son died, I'd sell the business, since it would have no appeal to me after that. For a little while, I think I even developed an irrational hostility toward BMWs.

Omar is a quiet, caring, and loving young man whom people often mistake for me. An outstanding football player, his six-foot-two-inch frame packs in 250 pounds. On the third anniversary (the exact month, day, and time) of his near-fatal accident, Omar was again in a horrific car crash.

I was at work; Lorna was on her way to the office when she got a call from a nurse who put Omar on the phone. He told his mother that he had been in an accident the night before and that he was going to have surgery. At first, we weren't scared. After all, he was able to talk to Lorna, so that made us feel as if it was just another freak accident and that he would be fine. In any case, we immediately rushed off to Westchester Medical Center to visit him and see his condition.

It felt as though we had just been there for the first accident. Upon arrival, there was confusion, and we saw people all around, crying. I remember hearing my daughter Monique and others saying that one of them had died, but nobody was mentioning a name.

I was frightened to think that it may have been Omar, but held on to the knowledge that he had just spoken with his mother at around eight that morning. Eventually, we were able to ascertain that both Omar and another good friend, the driver of the car, were seriously hurt, suffering from broken hips, pelvises, and other parts of their bodies.

The night had begun with several college students, along with a few of my nephews, eating fried chicken and celebrating the approaching end of summer and the start of a new school year. They were looking forward to going back to their colleges and universities in the fall. Of course, the celebrations consisted of the boys having a few beers and enjoying themselves. But the driver of the car had had one too many, and his actions would forever change the lives of three young men. The car crashed into a tree south of Route 22 in Scarsdale, New York. One of the young men, my son's best friend, had succumbed to his injuries.

It was a painful experience for me to attend the funeral of Omar's friend, knowing I was keeping the truth of his death away from my son as he recuperated from serious injuries. At the time, I thought it would be best if Omar didn't know about the boy's passing. Omar would lose two friends to the experience, one to death, the other to the penal system on a DWI conviction.

I cannot myself imagine the pain these young men feel. Omar seldom discusses the events of that August night, but I know how much it has affected him, as he internalizes much of the emotions from the ordeal. We continue to pray for his friend's family and seek God's guidance for all of them, even though I am sure this unfortunate accident was a lesson learned by the surviving boys. The driver has served his time and has since been baptized, and is contributing meaningfully to society. To God be the Glory; even in the midst of death He used the occasion to bring others to His throne.

Once again recovered and rehabilitated, my son still walks with a limp, but keeps going. That's Omar. To this day, I obsessively tell my children to drive carefully every time they're about to get into a motor vehicle.

* * *

Two years after Omar's first near-tragedy, the entire family would experience the moment we all knew was inevitable but would have done anything to postpone.

It came suddenly on May 25, 2006, when Ephraim Nathaniel Hawthorne, the patriarch of the family, passed away. We had made no emotional preparation for his passing. He had been such a rock for both our family and his home community of Border that no one contemplated a time when he would not be there.

As a former regular in the U.S. Farm Worker Program, Papa had always been a physically strong man who managed to look much younger than his years. He had proudly stood by me when I accepted my Order of Distinction from Jamaica's Governor General, Sir Howard Cooke, at the National Heroes' Day Awards in October 2005. He seemed fine when he attended the Jamaica Bakers' Association banquet for the first time after so many years in the business. Within days of that event, he was gone.

I temporarily lost my appetite for business. My advisor and sounding board, my foundation, was no more. Papa had been on spot when Easter bun season rolled around; he was also there, sitting quietly and leaning forward on his cane, when we did a photo shoot to promote Golden Krust restaurant meals. Then, just like that, he wasn't around anymore, and it felt as if my gut had been ripped out. Only recently, as I began to work on this book, have I started to think of myself as a successor, a family patriarch even. That will take many more years to sink in, because I still feel as if I sometimes defer to him in the abstract.

For the first time in my life, it was entirely clear that I was no longer just the baker's son, but my own man on an amazing business adventure. On the first anniversary of his death, I left work in the middle of the day to briefly forsake commerce and to memorialize him. His shadow is still so powerful.

CHAPTER THIRTEEN
Sharing and Caring

My entrepreneur's journey began more than twenty years ago with a philosophy and principle still valid today: put people before profit. True to that ideal, Golden Krust has become a pillar of strength within all the communities we serve. The company has implemented faith-based initiatives in which we partner with churches to consistently give back toward their mission, based on money spent within our franchise system. We also take advantage of advertising opportunities in church publications, newsletters, and journals, a practice that has paid off tremendously within the faith-based community. I believe that for the most part, it is because of this kind of active outreach that our brand enjoys the success it does today. I believe that wholeheartedly.

Our charity extends well beyond the church. When we first opened our doors, I took the position that we would never refuse any organization that requested free cocktail patties. I must say it took my marketing team some time to get used to the idea! Yet from the very start, the company focused its efforts on helping out with the catering needs of schools, community organizations, social clubs, job seekers, and wellness programs wherever it could.

I have given a lot to the church for several reasons, some quite obvious. First, as a Christian, I truly believe that it's good to contribute financially to the work of the

Lord. Second, churches and their pastors can be the most loyal followers a business like ours could ever have. Third, churches in the communities we serve often host events, which can range from pastors' appreciation days and assistance for needy congregants, to various forms of fundraising. The relationship is symbiotic, since they and Golden Krust need each other.

The Bible declares: to whom much is given, much is required. So we feel it's our responsibility to comply, and we do it happily. One of the initiatives I've embraced as the chairman of the American Foundation for the University of the West Indies (AFUWI) is the campaign concept called Adopt-A-Student. I feel as though I am uniquely prepared to be the campaign's ambassador and I articulate my philosophy—the importance of giving back, particularly through education—to various business communities. In several of my talks with business leaders, here in the United States as well as in Jamaica, I've said that if we are going to be successful we must embrace the younger generation, not only financially but also by giving in kind. My message to individuals and organizations is simply that we must increase our commitment to services like internships and mentorships, similar to what Golden Krust has been doing in its own sphere for years.

As business owners, we can be catalysts for change—if we are determined to do so. At one of my first board meetings, I remember saying in my opening remarks, "I left Jamaica as a minibus driver and could not have attended university when I lived there. I may have even transported some of you around this table . . . Today I am grateful for the opportunity to serve one of the greatest institutions of the Caribbean." That is what this country is all about: giving people the opportunity to reach their full potential.

In 2006, President George W. Bush declared June Caribbean-American Heritage Month to honor the impact that individuals have made to the very fabric of the American society in every spectrum. Many Caribbean luminaries, along with successful businesses, have been honored and recognized for their contributions. I have been honored by numerous organizations during this special June observance. Recently, I was honored by the Westchester Board of Legislators in my own backyard. What made this even more special was that my good friend and mentor Dr. Roy Hastick was honored at the same event for the indelible mark he has made on Caribbean businesses as the CEO of the Caribbean American Chamber of Commerce and Industry (CACCI).

Golden Krust celebrates June as "Education Month" throughout the franchise system. At specially planned events, we invite schoolchildren from various communities to feast on our products, and to learn about Golden Krust and the importance of education.

Our franchises have also gotten involved and plan their own initiatives. New York franchisee Charmaine Golding, for example, hosted Education Month at her store in Westchester. She invited in senior students from Woodlawn High School, and spoke quite candidly about the importance of education in their lives. At one of these special events, my youngest son Daren, a law student by this time, joined us onstage and said something so profound that I was taken aback.

"I could have taken the easy way out," he said to the students on that beautiful spring morning under the GK canopy with the sun in his face, "and jump into the family business and get a pretty good position. But I chose education. Business can disappear anytime, but a solid and good education stays with you forever." I was truly moved by his openness and sincerity.

For GK, June also means that for all crusts (baked plain crust without filling) that are sold within the system, 100 percent of the proceeds is put toward education. Some of our stores' cashiers and managers, as well as our marketing team, get into the celebration by wearing graduation attire for the occasion. Our slogan for the month is *Eat for the Cause*.

GK has been supplying New York City schools with Jamaican patties since 1996. These, however, are not the same as the ones sold in our franchise system. The school version is less spicy and are manufactured in strict adherence to the nutritional requirements instituted by local school boards and federal regulations.

Over the years, we have been able to gain a whole new cross-section of consumers through the school system—mainstream clientele. Like real estate, food franchising is a location business, but it also requires that the loyal customer base be replenished with like-minded individuals from the next generation. The reverse is also true: once children have had patties, they let their parents know about them, keeping the cycle of attraction and demand going in that fashion.

Care is taken to ensure that Golden Krust locations are as close to schools as possible, serving elementary, high, and trade schools, as well as colleges and universities. Many of our franchisees also support the idea of actively marketing to students by providing free meals for high achievers.

Golden Krust has not only invested heavily to promote healthy habits in the schools, but has also been a very strong proponent of higher education. The company has given computers to numerous schools to ensure that the next generation understands the importance of technology, and by extension, education.

The company has also given many scholarships to students in Jamaica and the United States. At Oberlin High, my alma mater in Jamaica, for example, Golden Krust has awarded numerous scholarships since 1999. The key point here is not the amounts given but the ability to motivate and inspire the children; they too can achieve with their God-given abilities if they put heart and soul behind their efforts. What we have done at Oberlin has raised the bar of optimism tremendously and fostered a competitive spirit among all the students there.

I try not to pass up any opportunity to speak at school events or commencement ceremonies. There are so many of these opportunities and we try to participate as much as time allows. And so we spread ourselves across dozens of scholastic and community events. On numerous occasions, I have had my son Omar, my siblings, or other top managers represent the company at these important engagements.

As our caring and giving increased over the years and the critical social needs of our loyal customer base became more visible, it dawned on me that we needed to formalize the charitable arm of the organization. Without hesitation, we named the new nonprofit entity after our parents. The Mavis & Ephraim Hawthorne Golden Krust Foundation was established in 2005 to contribute to multiple programs and charities throughout the United States and the islands of the Caribbean. The foundation is committed to:

- Developing a constituency to support the betterment of the community at large through scholarships,

social services, wellness programs, and activities.
- Creating and implementing programs and services.
- Influencing the development, adoption, and implementation of specific core curricula at secondary and tertiary institutions.
- Achieving economic viability that is grounded in a diversified funding base.

We established a board of directors that would keep core values at heart and bring individual professional and life experience to the foundation's mission. I serve as chairman, with my sister Lorraine as treasurer and sister-in-law Herma as secretary. Doctors Patricia Miller-Spencer, Desreene Freeman, and Romelle Maloney—all with their own personal histories connected to Golden Krust—were joined by Tanika Campbell as directors at large.

Before establishing the foundation, we had explored different concepts geared at generating revenue to fund our charitable endeavors. One of the ideas implemented was called Pennies for Change. The program gave our customers the opportunity to donate spare change left over from purchases at any of our GK locations. The goal was for each store to collect at least three dollars a day to go toward the foundation's efforts. Three dollars a day from all the Golden Krust locations adds up.

In 2006, one week before my father passed away, I went to Jamaica and presented him with the foundation logo, which features his and my mother's likenesses. I explained that the symbol would brand the philanthropic arm of the organization. Papa gave it his blessing. At the time, I also gave him and my stepmother, Sister Pat, the official invitation to the launch of the foundation, which was to have the distinguished patronage of Professor Gordon Shirley, then Jamaica's ambassador to the United States. The experience was extremely rewarding for Lorna, my siblings, and me, and filled us with a great sense of pride and accomplishment.

After my father's death, the family debated whether or not to go ahead with the staging of the scheduled foundation event. We realized that it would be potentially a very painful time for the family, but we moved forward nonetheless, knowing that the values of education and wellness lying at the core of the organization were so important to my parents. Without question, they would have told us to follow through.

On June 19, 2006, the glittering launch event was marked by the awarding of scholarships to nine outstanding students. I watched my brother Milton cry as he listened to excerpts of speeches given by my father over the years. He wasn't the only one with moist eyes as Papa's words were read. All of us had a fresh memory of his funeral held in Jamaica just two weeks earlier.

Although my father was gone, his presence could be felt all around the hall. I vividly remember the red and blue wall-to-wall banner with my father's picture, covering more than twenty feet, hanging above the podium. It read, *You can do all things through Christ Jesus who strengthens you.* It was easily one of his favorite sayings and has become a family motto of sorts.

Today, the foundation continues to grow, not just as a strong advocate for education, but as a promoter of other wellness programs. Once every year, we change the color of Golden Krust chicken patty bags to pink to help spread awareness about breast cancer and the need for screenings. In addition, we contribute a percentage of sales from the patties toward the American Cancer Society to fund research that will help win the fight against the dreaded illness. Under the auspices of the foundation, we have also worked with health institutions involved in prostate cancer research and other related programs.

Golden Krust has an endowment at Bronx Community College that provides financial assistance to at least five students every year. We recently signed a contract with the University of the West Indies to provide full scholarships to fifteen students over the next eight years. Now that I am chairman of the American Foundation for the University of the West Indies Partnership Board, I intend to continue to marshal as many resources as I can to the task of enhancing UWI's mission.

GK franchisees have also caught the philanthropic bug and, in their own way, are making a difference in various spheres. One GK proprietor, Jeffrey Reid, has built a computer lab and makes at least ten scholarships available each year for the Denham Town Primary School in west Kingston, Jamaica.

As chairman of the Mavis & Ephraim Hawthorne Foundation, I am extremely proud to be able to bring franchisees and our customers together under the idea that we should invest in education and the welfare of our people. Over the next few years as the company diversifies, I will heighten my own efforts to continue building this entity named in honor of my parents to expand their legacy. I will also be focusing on helping to establish franchising programs at the college level that will fuel the entrepreneurial spirit of our young people. I've discovered that a disproportionately low number of academic offerings are dedicated to franchising, even though this kind of enterprise is so significant to Americans and to overall job and wealth creation in America. Being a catalyst for specialized education in the field could help create a standard of qualification in our industry, leaving a success template for generations to come.

There will never be enough words to express my profound sense of pride when the City University of New York, through Medgar Evers College, chose to confer upon me an honorary doctor of letters degree in 2011.

In making the announcement, Medgar Evers College President Dr. William L. Pollard said, "We are pleased to be able to honor individuals of such distinguished character and achievement at the convocation ceremony. They truly reflect the highest standards to which our college aspires."

For me and my family, the news came as a culmination of all I have done over the years to instill the value of education at home, in my organization, and in the various associations and charities with which I am involved. The first thought I had was that Mama and Pops were not here to share my moment of absolute joy.

CHAPTER FOURTEEN
Faith's Awesome Power

It was with a sense of achievement and confidence in the future that the entire Hawthorne family welcomed 2009. In the twenty years that had passed since we opened our first store at 1381 East Gun Hill Road, the remarkable progress of Golden Krust was indeed a cause for celebration among family and friends. In just eight years after opening our doors, we were granted our franchise license, and with the expansion of our operations in the New York tri-state area, we were well on our way to becoming America's foremost Caribbean brand.

The son of a rural village in central Jamaica had certainly come a long way toward realizing his American Dream. Such was the aura of success Golden Krust generated that we all assumed that our most formidable challenges were behind us. It was against this backdrop of achievement and expectation that a personal crisis tested my faith in no uncertain manner. No one would have guessed that before the end of the year, the euphoria of success would give way to pain and sorrow as sudden illness brought me to the brink of eternity. Only the tight circle of family and friends would know the deep valleys through which I would pass before a miracle brought me back to life and health.

Through it all, I lost neither faith nor hope, and I attribute this in no small way to the grounding in Christian values I received from my parents, my faith in the never-failing love of the Almighty, the power of fervent prayer, and the fellowship of my church community.

Looking back, I have to conclude that in all my trials and tribulations, God was working His purpose, and had chosen me to be a witness of His grace and favor. Whereas I had already experienced several crises which had forced me to contemplate the loss of those nearest and dearest to me, the third would bring me face-to-face with my own mortality.

January 11, 2009 started like any other Sunday morning, a marker for a new week in my life. I had just returned from Jamaica with Lorna and Daren, my youngest, where we had celebrated New Year's with a lot of good cheer and optimism. It was a bit humid and unseasonably warm. After giving thanks to God for His saving grace and the dawn of a new day, I joined Lorna, who was downstairs preparing a tuna sandwich and a seriously strong cup of Jamaican Blue Mountain coffee. At the table, I prayed that God would continue to surround my children and my extended family with His love and protect them in all that they did.

Being a spiritual man, I have always wanted to have my children in church with me. I believe wholeheartedly in the principles and philosophies that my father shared, and so was determined to pass the same values on to my kids in turn. Words from my father like, "Follow after me as I follow after Christ" and "Be of good courage and walk as men" have been close to my heart since I was a boy. I truly believe that creating the same environment for my children that my father did for my siblings and me would lead them to Christ, ultimately transforming their lives and placing Him at the center of their joy.

I had invited Haywood, Omar, and Monique to accompany me to church. Daren had already returned to college.

I wanted to get the New Year rolling with the idea that as long as you are in church, God's presence will wash over you. That being said, I had chosen that morning to try something different and visit Grace Baptist Church in Mt. Vernon for Sunday service. This church has thousands of members, lots of young people, a vibrant youth choir, and many who have been able to break the barriers of inequality to achieve success in several fields. I consider Grace Baptist an institution that deeply cares for and represents the best interests of African-Americans. I also thought this congregation may be the best fit for my kids since they didn't regularly go with me to the Church of the Nazarene in Westchester.

There was a great feeling of the spirit that morning. I was so happy that everyone at home was on a mission to attend worship. Monique went ahead to my brother's church in the Bronx; Omar promised that he would join us at Grace later. Looking forward to a great Sunday, we set out. Haywood rode in the front with me; Lorna sat in the backseat.

We arrived at Grace Baptist at about eleven twenty a.m. The service had just begun and the choir was already in full voice, so our plan was to quietly slip in and be seated. At the entrance, I stretched my hand out to an usher to get a copy of the day's bulletin. Just then, I felt an excruciating pain—something I've never felt before or since—beginning at the forehead and shooting straight to the back of my head. I became immediately concerned because I was never someone you could classify as a headache sufferer. I had no idea what a migraine might feel like, since I'd never had one before.

Something had to be radically wrong with my body. Despite the pain, I proceeded to the pews to take my seat and joined in the singing of the well-known hymn "Amazing Grace." The harmonious voices of the choir, the congregation, and the senior pastor, Reverend Franklin Richardson, echoed through the church in a thrilling melody that would stay with me throughout my predicament. The words of the second stanza—'*T'was Grace that taught my heart to fear, / And Grace, my fears relieved; / How precious did that Grace appear / The hour I first believed*—were a source of great comfort, and just what I needed to hear at that moment. I tried to focus on the song in the hymnal, keeping the crippling sensation to myself, hoping it would pass.

I began to pray quietly, still singing the hymn. As the pain worsened, I nudged Lorna.

"I'm having a really bad headache," I managed to say through my teeth. Once I got Haywood's attention, I mentioned it to him as well. I must have appeared to them simply as Dad with a regular headache, because they didn't appear to have any idea what was happening inside my skull. If they had, I'm sure they would have rushed me out of the building the way Secret Service agents whisk a U.S. president away from danger.

The pain persisted, but I stood up each time I was bidden and participated fully in the service. Somehow, I also kept looking out for Omar to arrive. There was no sign of him. The pain reached the point where I said to Lorna, "I need to find some pain medication—this pain is getting really bad."

Then I just got up and walked, half-crazed by the colossal headache, hunting for painkillers like a man possessed, still wondering why Omar hadn't shown up.

Finding myself in the cafeteria, I asked the cashier for headache medicine; she said she had none. Heading back to the sanctuary, I saw two old ladies carrying enormous handbags. From what I knew about some old ladies and their bags, I knew they might have enough first aid to impress a paramedic. I began to ask if they had anything that could help, but the Lord must have whispered in my ear, urging me not to ask but to keep praying. You see, the worst thing you can possibly do is to take aspirin while suffering from a brain hemorrhage.

Rejoining the congregation, I saw Haywood clapping, dancing, and enjoying the worship so much that I ignored the pain and rejoiced in his celebration, eventually staying for the entire service. Afterward, I described the episode to Haywood and Lorna. For good or ill, I decided to drive home instead of letting my wife or son drive me. With my years of driving experience, I did so out of habit—and the feeling that I could navigate through the potholes more expertly.

Once home, I went straight to bed with pain still ripping through my head. I remember hearing crowd sounds from my TV. The Giants and Eagles were locked in an NFL playoff battle, but I just couldn't focus, no matter how much I wanted to see the game. I tried sleeping, but to no avail. It was only at this point that I began to form the idea that my health was in serious peril, but I quickly banished the thought. After all, I was only forty-eight, father of four, a successful family man with a wife I loved and cherished. *This can't be happening to me . . .*

Once again, I began to pray quietly.

Then, as if guided by some force outside myself, I asked Lorna, Monique, and Haywood to accompany me to West-chester Medical Center. I drove the car to the emergency room and hurriedly tried to locate a parking spot close to the entrance. Thankfully I found one. At the registration desk, it was I who politely stood at the counter in my Sunday best, completing all the required hospital forms and answering questions. Matter-of-factly, a nurse took my blood pressure. She said it was slightly elevated but there was no cause for alarm. I'm convinced that her feeling was prompted by my positive attitude and calm spirit, not medical procedure. I imagine God tapped her on the shoulder and recommended a CAT scan even though deep down she may have thought it unnecessary.

I sat on a bed in the emergency room, patiently waiting to be wheeled to the radiology department for the CAT scan. I got there and stayed quiet. Everything was a typically neutral experience until I realized that the technician's face showed something ominous. Either something had gone wrong procedurally with the test or I was about to confront my biggest nightmare. At the time, I was afraid to ask for any kind of result.

Slowly, they moved me into the room where my family was waiting. In about fifteen minutes, I noticed movement among doctors and nurses. That's when I was sure I was in trouble.

A doctor came over to us. "Mr. Hawthorne," he said briskly, "you've suffered an aneurysm."

They say that at times like this, your life flashes before you. Instead, it was more like I saw the lives of other people who had survived this type of ordeal. Vice President Joe Biden came to mind; then I saw my father, who had passed away just three years earlier from a ruptured aneurysm. Before thinking about how the hospital might help me, I knew that faith in God and my will to live would pull me through. Even so, I asked again, *Why me?*

Lying flat on the bed, I opened my eyes. Monique and Lorna were standing over me. It was then, as my eyes met theirs, that I began to panic. For what turned out to be nearly a half hour, my body trembled uncontrollably. My wife and daughter tried their best to calm me but their efforts brought no relief.

At some point—I'm not entirely sure when—a young nurse came over, placed her hand on my forehead, and whispered softly near my ear, "Mr. Hawthorne, you're going to be okay . . . You're in one of the best hospitals, with one of the best medical teams." Some measure of calm returned to my spirit when she said, "This is a procedure that is done a thousand times here. You're in good hands." *Good hands.* I had to believe that God's good hands would lift me up.

Lucid again, I immediately asked Lorna to notify my pastor and the rest of the family of what had happened to me. Within minutes, family members began pouring in. A prayer vigil was initiated, fervently seeking a miraculous healing touch. Pastor came by and prayed. Lorna also got a hold of Daren at American University. It had to be a bad time for him to come home so soon after the new semester had begun. Regardless, I just knew I wanted him at my bedside to complete the family circle with all hands joined.

By early morning, the word had gone out to the franchising community and to several churches, both in the U.S. and the Caribbean. It was in the local newspapers, on the radio, and in other media. There were differing reports on exactly what my situation was. I'm told there were rumors that I had died.

Prayer warriors from all denominations and faiths began to pray for my recovery in earnest. The business community, especially Golden Krust franchisees, had no way to tell what was going to happen to me—or, for that matter, what was to become of the empire that I had built.

The fact was, I was in the intensive care unit at Westchester Medical—and that was alarming enough. Friends and folks from all over wanted to visit me there, but Lorna marshaled the doors, ensuring that no one entered unless authorized by her. She wanted me to get all the rest I needed. Hawthornes and Morrisons kept coming, and by my estimate, we must have had at least thirty-five people in the room praying, singing, and praising God. It seemed as if the ward had been transformed into a sanctuary.

Songs of praise permeated the room:

Your grace and mercy brought me through
I'm living this moment because of You
I want to thank You, and praise You too

I began to cry and surrender my life to Jesus anew. I trusted even more that He would deliver me if I rested all my burdens at His feet. We prayed that God would perform a miracle in my life, to make this whole experience yet another testimony of God's grace, favor, and love for the human race. I had the entire night, until tests were performed in the morning, to find out if He had listened or if I was living out my last moments.

After a night of prayer, we got a measure of good news. Doctors did an angiogram, the procedure in which they shoot dye into your veins and take an X-ray to see any abnormalities on a scope or screen. They found no further bleeding. This was all good news, and the doctors decided they would perform another similar test within the next four days.

In the meantime, more family members began to arrive: my sisters Jackie, from Georgia, and Cassandra and her family; my brother Lloyd, who flew in from Florida to pray with me and comfort me. I consider those six days in the hospital the longest days in my life, but with strong family ties and faith in God, I was able to hold on.

The second angiogram showed no evidence of aneurysm either. "To God be the glory, great things he has done!" I declared. By now, blood from my hemorrhage had drained to my spine, causing excruciating pain that almost crippled me. For the first two weeks, I couldn't get out of bed or walk without assistance. I recall my nephew Andre giving me a daily massage; Herma, my physical therapist sister-in-law, also spent many an evening working on my legs.

My nieces Desrene and Marcia were more doctor than nurse. Marcia was there for me around the clock. Lorna would take turns, as did my lovely mother-in-law Hyacinth. They had taken time off from work or left their families to be with me for weeks. Their mission was to make sure I got the right food, as well as the correct dosages of medication prescribed.

In the end, the official diagnosis of my condition was sub-arachnoid hemorrhage (SAH), bleeding in the brain caused by an aneurysm. They say you can identify the onset of SAH by what's called a "thunderclap headache," which feels like you've been kicked in the skull, moving in a pulsating manner to the back of the head. Technically a kind of stroke, 50 percent of SAH cases are fatal. Many of those who survive have some amount of brain damage and cognitive impairment. I'd survived on one-to-one odds.

After a few weeks, I was convalescing at home. Slowly, I began walking again. In all, I was laid up at home for almost two months, which is exactly two months longer than I ever thought I could be away from Golden Krust with no involvement in the business. Today, because of my miracle, I have no residual effects of the episode.

Back at GK headquarters, everything ran without a hitch. I had set up an effective succession plan to ensure continuity no matter what happened. My son Haywood, who is executive vice president, my sister Lorraine, and other members of the team rose to the occasion and carried out the daily operations of the company.

Since my health scare, I feel I have a closer relationship with Christ, drawing even closer to Him than before. For me, this sensation is more than a cliché; it's what I'm living.

I now even have a closer relationship with my wife and children. Priorities change. Now it's Christ first, then health and family, personal things in life, then business, and so on, in that order. And it is true what they say: success, fame, and money mean nothing if you don't have good health. Today, I spend a lot of time building the Mavis & Ephraim Hawthorne Foundation, serving as a mentor to young people, and focusing on my children. I want them to have the best chance to be great future parents and leaders. Of course, Lorna and I are also doing things for the love of life, such as tennis, beginner golf, or just traveling the world. Thanks be to God that His presence keeps watching over us.

CHAPTER FIFTEEN
The Path to the Future

Our crazy idea of Golden Krust becoming a Caribbean food juggernaut has come true, surpassing even our wildest dreams. Without question, the brand has become a major force to be reckoned with among quick-serve restaurants (QSR), and every day the GK vision grows sharper. Today, Golden Krust is considered a major player in our business category. Systemwide sales in 2010 were estimated to exceed $100 million and are poised to continue on a growth path. Our current trajectory could take annual revenues past $500 million by 2020.

Though franchising has given the company widespread brand recognition, publicity, and, of course, a profit center, it is also the retail channel through which the brand will be able to go national in a meaningful way. As far as we've come, and as well known as the Golden Krust name is to those seeking a taste of the Caribbean, our beloved flavors and foods are not yet truly mainstream. Ask anyone with Jamaican or West Indian heritage and chances are s/he has heard of us; ask anyone else and they've heard of McDonald's. That's the kind of position we'd like to be in ten years from now, where GK is more of a regular choice at the upper end of demand. Not so long ago, we started out wanting to be well known to Jamaicans and West Indians; then, it was to be chosen by lovers of the Caribbean flavor and vibe. Finally, we'll aim to be more top-of-mind with any consumer looking for a quick-service meal option—someone who is equally open to the top names in tacos, Southern fried chicken, or burgers and fries. Mainstream concept.

Well on our way to opening two hundred outlets in the United States, Golden Krust also has consumer products which are already established fare in many parts of the American penal system, in Costco stores, and several supermarkets on the East Coast. But where expansion was dependent on signing new franchisees, the road ahead will be the diversification route, moving the brand aggressively from the storefront into the home pantry.

The growth of GK, therefore, lies beyond the franchise concept, through retail and even real estate channels. As a franchisor, the company holds numerous leases on its outlet locations. Gradually, and as conditions allow, we will acquire an increasing number of deeds to these properties, securing the physical positioning of the outlets and achieving optimal management over their cost of operations. In addition, we are unique in our positioning as a manufacturer, not a reseller, of products sold in the outlets. As a result, we have more control over the factors of production, and franchisees are less affected by fluctuations in the price of (and markup placed upon) raw materials. The additional 30,000 square feet of manufacturing space being added to our Bronx headquarters will mean a near-tripling of our capacity from 300 to 850 patties a minute. At that rate, we'll sell our billionth patty in a few years, having already come halfway toward that milestone.

Long before talk about food security became fashionable, Golden Krust was already staggering the supply of our flagship product in the millions through offsite locations so as to guarantee uninterrupted supply to both GK restaurants and retail outlets. We will continue to add facilities that build more redundancy into the overall operation in case of disaster.

As I write this, the company is entering the consumer retail market for items such as sauces, fruit juice, coconut water, and other products that resonate with our overall vision. The move will allow Golden Krust to develop different profit centers by capitalizing on the brand equity built over the years from the first shop in the Bronx to the network of franchised locations and sales to institutions, wholesale shopping clubs, and beyond. Going full bore into retail branding is no picnic, however. One of the things that first struck me about the supermarket business was, well, the cost of doing business in the supermarket. You have to pay what's called slotting fees, which sometimes can run into the thousands of dollars depending on the supermarket chain you want to sell in.

Sometimes called pay-to-stay fees, they are charged to manufacturers by retailers to get their product on the shelves. A basic fee for a new product may be about $25,000 per item as a regional fee, but can rise to several times that figure in bigger markets.

Product development will be the key to the success of the brand going forward. During that process, I'm ready to put any product into our famous crust that might be marketable to the mainstream.

Over the last few years, I have eased away from the basic operations of the company. I believe that when you've been immersed in the day-to-day activities for so long, it can prevent you from focusing on the big picture. For the vision to be realized, others are now filling in where I no longer can. For example, my son Omar has been playing an increasingly crucial role in the company's public relations effort. Far more talented than I was at that age, he

188 // THE BAKER'S SON

has become an articulate face of the company, spending much of his time representing us at events throughout the U.S. and overseas. Haywood, my eldest, focuses on the development of the brand, new products, and running the manufacturing operation—an executive vice president in every sense of the word.

Though my focus at GK is more on macro than micro aspects of the master plan, I am still very proactive and detail oriented in whatever I'm doing. Sometimes, the detail gets very fine: I have already begun, for instance, to think of the implications of Golden Krust's impact in 2020. Will Jamaica—or the entire Caribbean for that matter—be able to produce enough thyme, pepper, and other spices germane to creating a good Jamaican patty? Or consider this: the average cow carries about seven pounds of kidney fat (suet), the stuff that gives patties their leak-proof flakes in the crust. We currently use about 7,500 pounds a day. Will the suet so vital to our process be enough for such a market—or will we have to look at alternative ingredients? For the 2020 target, we're talking about 100,000 pounds of beef suet a day! We would need millions of pounds on the trot, and our own planes for transporting the indispensable thyme and Jamaican scotch bonnet peppers as well. Plans would have to be put in place to acquire hundreds of acres to farm these specialty ingredients, if we're going to meet the consumer's need for authentic taste at that not-too-distant time.

For both entrepreneurs and citizens of the world in general, 2008 will always be remembered for the worst financial collapse since 1929. Coming as it did after a boom in the global economy which had been sustained for over a decade, many failed to see the warning signs and were taken by surprise.

The unfolding events, which were for the most part unprecedented, included, according to Fareed Zakaria in his book *The Post-American World*:

The destruction of approximately fifty trillion dollars in assets in the global economy; the nationalization of America's largest mortgage lenders; the largest bankruptcy in history (Lehman Brothers); the disappearance of the investment bank; bailouts and stimulus packages around the world adding up to trillions of dollars.

In the United States, the devastation of the economy left a trail of bankruptcies. With the benefit of hindsight, we can now see more clearly that in the boom years an increasing number of Americans were left behind.

Between the 1990s and 2007, the top 1 percent of the richest Americans increased their share of the national income from 15 to 23 percent. With little or no movement in the wages of the middle and working classes, their lifestyles were increasingly financed by credit, and when the crash came, they had little or nothing in the form of savings on which to fall back. Inflated values and easy lending terms had created a housing "bubble" which was the first to burst, leading to "foreclosures and walk-aways, neighborhoods plagued by abandoned properties and plummeting home values," in the words of Barbara Kiviat in *Time* magazine. The latest estimate is that in the process, American homeowners lost some six trillion dollars in housing wealth.

The crisis was so deep that despite massive stimulus packages, real recovery is still some way off and jobs, even for many middle-class Americans, remain a hope more than a reality. The fact is that as long as large numbers

of the middle and working classes of America remain un-
employed, there will just not be the disposable income to
sustain consumer demand for the goods and services that
the U.S. economy is capable of producing. Without that
sustained demand, prospects for the kind of recovery that
the U.S. economy needs may not materialize for some time
to come.

While the American economy was being devastated
and business enterprises were failing, Golden Krust not
only survived, but thrived, adding franchises and value every year. Recognition of our sustained growth during this
challenging business period came on Sunday, August 23,
2009, when a large gathering of our friends and support-
ers joined us at the Living Word Community Church in
Lauderhill, Florida, to celebrate our twentieth anniversary.
One newspaper described Golden Krust as an "emergent
entrepreneurial global entity," observing that it was "extremely difficult to identify another Afrocentric family in the
Diasporas or throughout the Caribbean . . . with the vision
to transform this close-knit business into a conglomerate."

A second event had also made 2009 a watershed year,
one that profoundly shaped the way Americans viewed
themselves and the way the world viewed America: the
inauguration of Barack Obama as President of the United
States.

No one could have written the script as it unfolded. He
had certainly caught my attention on the night he spoke
at the 2004 Democratic National Convention which nomi-
nated John Kerry. There was definitely something special
about this newly elected senator from Chicago. But despite
the acclaim in the national press, I did not yet see a path to
the White House for him. Then came the primaries and the
tipping point in January 2008, when he decisively defeated

both Hillary Clinton and John Edwards in the Iowa Caucus. I still recall the passion with which he spoke that night and the inspiration that I as a black American entrepreneur drew from his words to Americans—of all races—who had voted for him. "You know, they said this day would never come," he declared. "They said our sights were set too high . . . but on this January night, at this defining moment in history, you have done what the cynics said we couldn't do . . . our time for change has come."

Some had dared to hope that the son of a black Kenyan and a white American would emerge as the Democratic Party's candidate for president. When he did, others began to dream a previously impossible dream. His victory at the polls and his inauguration as the forty-fourth President of the United States reverberated throughout the international community as no political event had done before, removing forever many limitations to the possibilities of people of African descent everywhere.

There are many memories of that election night that will always remain with me. One is the image of the Obama family: Barack, Michelle, and their two daughters, Malia and Sasha, as they walked out onto the stage at Grant Park in Chicago to be received to the tumultuous applause of the 125,000 people gathered there. It was a picture of the ideal family representing the best in American family values.

In 2008, when Michelle Obama delivered the keynote address on the first night of the Democratic National Convention, she reminded her audience that she and her husband lived by the creed "that you work hard for what you want in life; that your word is your bond and you do what you say you're going to do; that you treat people with dignity and respect, even if you don't know them, and even if you don't agree with them."

My mind went back to Papa and Mama and their superhuman effort to raise their family within a framework of Christian values and a sense of industry and cooperation. I also kept thinking that somewhere at Oberlin High School in Jamaica, there were students who with some assistance could also break barriers and create hope in a community where many live in despair. It increased my resolve to do everything I could to ensure that the Golden Krust Foundation would always make a difference.

CHAPTER SIXTEEN
Wealth, the Golden Krust Way

I've been asked by folks, when I do speaking engagements or when I meet them in my travels, how Golden Krust was able to build such a strong brand in such a short time from what started out as a humble neighborhood bakery. Some want to know what it's like working with so many family members. Others ask for the secret of how to get a kind of multiplier effect for their venture, a way to expand exponentially. Believe it or not, the last question is the easiest of the three to answer, because building a brand is by no means an easy task, especially a Caribbean brand in the United States of America. Our logo made up of sunrays adorned with different colors carries specific symbolic significance. The name Golden Krust represents the flaky crust for the signature patties. The golden sunrays represent the colors of the Caribbean and the bright sunshine of the islands.

GK's success truly began with product quality and product differentiation. We present a clear vision—taking the taste of the Caribbean to the world—and a mission that delivers that vision. I'd never tell a family to mortgage all their collective property, empty savings and investment accounts, and borrow from any friends who have a kind ear. But as the previous chapters show, that's what we did, because we had no shot at this type of success otherwise.

That kind of economics would have to be the exception, not the rule. Which is why I chose to use this final chapter to share my observations and ideas, the things that shaped me in business and formed my core.

We watched our first Golden Krust location gain in popularity and financial stability for a while before taking the franchise route. And as the GK brand moves in waves across America, I'm certain now that franchise success is more a combination of hard work and strategic planning than anything else. Of course, you need a good original and popular idea as a foundation, but there are great food concepts that are not franchised and so-so ones that are. Either way, I consider our wide reach and loyal customers a tremendous achievement in the face of challenges, obstacles, and constraints.

Our road to franchising the Golden Krust brand has not been an easy journey. Coming up from a modest family business to becoming a name spoken in the same breath as well-known QSR brands also comes with the same responsibilities these other major players in the industry have. A franchisor has, for example, to exercise great patience, tolerance, and an ability to deal with various personalities, while at the same time conducting business in a fair and ethical manner. So there's no simple secret, but there are definitely guidelines to follow and pitfalls to avoid.

Even for successful franchises, the relationship with the franchisees, the ones who carry the brand flag, can be bumpy. One of the things that struck me in this so-called "big boy club" of quick-service brands was how little empathy is felt for the franchisor by both franchisees and the legal system. To put it plainly, franchisees often depend on franchisors for every little thing, and expect franchisors to have solutions to all their problems. The result is that being a chain supplier, manufacturer—even landlord in some cases—makes it even more difficult to separate the franchisor from the franchisees who are supposed to be independent business owners. Yes, I am cognizant of the fact that GK depends on franchisees for a large slice of its revenue, but there comes a time when they have to learn to fly on their own. If they don't, then they're not really doing business.

I believe strongly in education for every field of endeavor. Amazingly, although more than 50 percent of American businesses are made up of some form of franchise concept, the subject is not a significant feature in higher education. Additionally, franchising makes up some 3 percent of our national GDP, yet it gets very short shrift in university programs. To fill some of that gap, we created a training center to teach new franchisees how to become great entrepreneurs, regardless of educational background. When we put new franchisees into our system, they must endure weeks of rigorous instruction at our training center to ensure that they get the tools and skills necessary to be a Golden Krust proprietor. Topics in the curriculum include Human Resources, Accounting, Hygiene, QSR Marketing, Sales and Merchandising, Cooking, Customer Service, Construction Management, and, of course, Food Presentation.

Golden Krust franchisees tend to become very successful entrepreneurs, and our first franchise holders are still at it, profitably, decades later. As a matter of fact, we were well past seventy locations before a single one was lost by an investor. That statistic strengthens my belief that good franchisees typically run a better operation than corporations would, due to the fact that they are hands-on with the day-to-day operation of the company and have a better handle on action and reaction in their fast-paced environments.

When Ted Knight started out peddling handmade running shoes from his car in Oregon, he was trying to sell his American alternative footwear in a market dominated by the German brands Adidas and Puma (founded by two brothers who once worked in the family shoe business before becoming rivals). What was at first mere potential turned into major sales growth over the ensuing years, until Nike became not just the world leader in sports goods, but an iconic cultural touchstone as well. Nike gear worn by Michael Jordan, Tiger Woods, and other celebrities propelled that company to its spot atop the mountain. After their earlier runaway leadership in the market, the two old German brands remain strong but now trail Nike. Additionally, as we've seen with the German example, there's no certainty or recipe for a family business to succeed, either. What is achievable, though, is running a good business.

It may sound obvious, but a company seeking brand success has to create distinction and separation from the competition using its name as a key business representative, sort of a unique front door. Branding experts will tell you that in an environment dominated by some very strong brands, the power of the trademark itself, not the physical products, serves as a formidable barrier to challengers.

There were tremendous risks and of course possibilities for litigation to franchise a name that is not trademarked. Basic Franchise Rule 101: if you don't own it, you can't franchise it. This was the case with Golden Krust. We learned through our attorney that we did not own the name we had used for seven years. Despite this predicament, we had no plans to slow down the process of becoming a franchisor.

Once we found out we changed the name from Golden Krust Caribbean Bakery to Golden Krust Patties, a name we rightly owned. Personally, I did not like the name Golden Krust Patties because it would limit us and cause us to be perceived as a patty operation rather than a full QSR. Having no choice, we proceeded accordingly. I met with my team and family members and devised a plan to secure the Golden Krust name. We appointed a member of the team, Al Alston, to lead the charge. I thought he was the best person for the job. He was young, black, articulate with a Southern accent, and he possessed a respectful and calm demeanor.

Al had joined the police pension section of NYPD in 1985. He was always well dressed and he came from a well-knit family like ours. His upbringing was rooted in strong Christian principles. Al had spent many years working with Merrill Lynch prior to joining the NYPD. When I was contemplating leaving the NYPD, he was one of the people who tried to convince me to move on to corporate America, since he himself was a product of Wall Street. I told him that I could not afford to take on the uncertainty of Wall Street, being a family man, and given the cutthroat business practices.

Al parted company with the NYPD after four years and went to work for Bear Stearns, a Wall Street giant. We stayed in touch, and Al became one of my key sounding boards for the bakery establishment. When the time came for me to hire an accountant, Al was an easy pick. He was later promoted to director of franchise sales and played a pivotal role in our growth. Today, he is the proud owner of three Golden Krust franchises in Queens, New York.

But back in 1996, when dealing with the matter of starting a franchise, we asked Al for help. Basically, we asked him to travel to Cohoes, New York, to visit the establishment that shared our name and report his findings back to us. This was a gutsy move—here we were, sending a representative to meet with the owners, a man and his wife, who had been in business for over fifty years (approximately ten years before I was born), armed with the message that we needed to use their business name.

On the morning in question, a Tuesday, Al set out from Queens, heading 160 miles north, arriving in Cohoes at about ten a.m. He drove around the area, trying to get a feel for this other "Golden Krust" operation. Al would call me with an update every fifteen minutes. The first breakthrough came when he rang to tell me that the business seemed quite small, practically a "hole in the wall." Al then ventured inside, introduced himself, and requested to speak with the owners. He was under strict instructions not to divulge our franchising plans or the number of locations we operated under the Golden Krust name. After a couple hours of negotiations, while feasting on stuffed cabbage and bagels, Al called with the good news: the owners were willing to give us the rights to use the name, and also rights of first refusal should we consider purchasing their business.

That day's deal was sealed with a gentleman's handshake. We secretly celebrated the scaling of that hurdle, but in the back of our minds we were concerned that the owner might renege on the promise. After a few weeks of further negotiations and the drafting of legal documents, the owners signed the deal, selling us the rights to use the name, thereby releasing us to develop franchises.

No sooner had new celebrations begun when we discovered that someone else owned a business named "Golden Krust" in Florida. This was a big surprise! And it was a much larger operation: a manufacturer of Jamaican patties with a large USDA manufacturing plant. We knew that getting the owners to the table was not going to be easy, but we were very determined. Our investigation revealed that the business was owned by a couple named Roland and Rose, who also operated a club called Crystal in Fort Lauderdale. Our purchasing the operation was for them an opportunity to get out of the baking business, as Roland was suffering from poor health.

Unlike the owners of Golden Krust in Cohoes, however, Roland had done his due diligence and found out about our intention to expand into Florida. This information he used to his advantage, making the negotiation much harder than we had anticipated. (Roland would not live long enough to know that the bakery he and his wife sold us with such confidence, joy, and pride would fail miserably.)

Again I gathered my team to discuss strategy, and we decided that this time it would be best for me to lead this charge. My plan was to go in with an offer too good to refuse. Arriving in Fort Lauderdale with our CPA, Alfred Simms, we conducted our assessment and quickly concluded that it was perfect for our purposes. It already had a lot of equipment and was USDA certified—this was the opportunity of a lifetime, we thought.

Despite the great deal of money we had to spend in the process, we managed to close the deal, finally acquiring the Golden Krust name in Florida and freeing us to implement our expansion strategy. The facility was quite large, with eighteen staff members and three delivery trucks. We immediately relocated our sales director Desrene and other members of the management staff to take over the operation. The celebration, however, was short lived. The business was a monumental failure.

In assessing our losses, we concluded that a growing company cannot build manufacturing plants in multiple locations. A business like the one we had acquired could only remain viable with a number of distribution channels to support it, along with a low-cost structure and strong profit margins. To date, this has been the company's biggest loss. After two years of operations, we closed shop and redirected our focus on development in New York. We disassembled equipment, packed our wares, and said our goodbyes. On that fateful day I remember saying to the team, "I will be back." Looking back at this experience reminds us of the words of the popular Kenny Rogers song which says, *"Know when to walk away, know when to run . . ."*

Three years to the date of this closure, we reentered the Florida market, this time armed with more sophisticated strategic and marketing plans and, most importantly, with our mouth-watering patties and home-style meals. Even though Florida has the second-largest Caribbean population in the U.S. (after New York), this was no easy feat. Other Jamaican restaurant concepts like Island Grill had come to Florida and failed miserably. Yet our experience has taught us that if we are to become the industry leader, we must make it in Florida.

One of the things we did differently on our second entry was to establish a minibakery to produce bread and other pastry products—with my oldest brother Lloyd, a master baker, at the helm. He would control that aspect of the distribution while patties and marinated chicken would be shipped from New York.

Not long after this reentry, we opened our first Florida franchise with Lovett Miller, a well-respected Fort Lauderdale businesswoman. This was a great sign of what was to come. Today at GK, Florida rivals New York, with over twenty stores and plans to open fifty others within the next three years.

We know that great food in the right location for the right market always does well, but there are times when we have to admit that someone else's product tastes good. By honestly reporting our research findings on the competition we are able, if necessary, to make the changes that effectively improve what we offer to our customers. I've often worn dark glasses, a hat, and sometimes even dreadlocks to go undercover and eat, shop, or just walk around neighborhoods and check on the competition, just to see for myself how they measure up. In order to facilitate constant research on and monitoring of the opposition, my sales staff has been given the green light to buy any product of a new business so that a taste test can be done immediately.

Undeniably, Golden Krust's success has been strengthened by Jamaican ethnocentric culinary habits. We also stand to benefit from a welcome shift in the tastes of Hispanics, Haitians, Eastern Caribbean-American nationals, and others who now enjoy the tasty delights offered by our outlets.

Golden Krust has not yet deeply penetrated the college campuses and high schools in the U.S. as we have witnessed with Kentucky Fried Chicken and the other indigenous fast food conglomerates. We are still putting together the corporate strategies required to set us on par with the best of our peers in the quick-serve business. We are quite confident that Golden Krust can achieve financial success similar to that of several other major fast food brands. This is validated by our recent federal disclosure documents, which show that 26 percent of Golden Krust stores have generated revenue in excess of a million dollars and another

25 percent in excess of $750,000. This is, of course, far better than many OSRs in this country. If you compare our sales levels to those of major players, particularly Burger King, KFC, Subway, and Quiznos, GK is on par with or ahead of them in terms of same-store sales.

We now know the returns from an investment of time and energy in selecting the best locations for siting our restaurants. This, along with economical price points for small kiosk–type restaurants and irresistible food, will enable us to capture and retain a strong customer base. In 1989, we walked and drove up and down the Bronx searching for an ideal location to launch the business. We quickly learned that the most optimal spot to site a new Golden Krust, particularly in New York, was at a busy subway station entrance. This was the approach that Starbucks and other brands have used to such good effect. It was for this reason that the Gun Hill Road site was so important to us and also why the owner who sold it to us did everything to maximize his profit on the sale!

We have found that ideal New York locations are not limitless, and so in true and innovative GK style, we've had to create more room. For smaller-than-average outlay, potential franchisees can now operate a Golden Krust Kiosk/Express design layout in locations between three hundred and six hundred square feet. Since the franchise fee is only $15,000, and with an estimated initial investment that ranges from just under $185,000 to just over $300,000, the smaller, high-traffic locations can be used for spreading the Golden Krust magic, not just for the palates of customers, but also for the fortunes of new franchisees from all walks of life. The Golden Krust Express concept has been moving into shopping malls, colleges, hospitals, airport terminals, and similar locations.

In the summer of 2008, "Brand Jamaica" received a major boost at the Beijing Olympic Games. The year before these games, Jamaica had established itself as an athletics superpower, with Asafa Powell and Sherone Simpson topping the international rankings for both men and women in the 100-meter race. When the gold medals were tallied in Beijing, Jamaican sprinters Usain Bolt, the "pocket-rocket" Shelly-Ann Fraser, Veronica Campbell-Brown, Kerron Stewart, Powell, Simpson, and others were the toast of the Olympics.

The identification of Golden Krust with the growing visibility and vitality of Jamaica as a brand creates an ideal platform for leveraging the fame of our Olympians as spokespersons for the GK conglomerate in North America and Europe. This is the next fertile arena for the inevitable expansion of GK's franchise package and for penetration into the Asian, European, and hemispheric American markets as well.

At the end of the day, West Indians remain our primary market segment. For this reason, we rely heavily on their desire for that heavenly smelling oxtail, jerk pork, jerk chicken, escoveitch fish, or their choice of eight varieties of the Jamaican patty. Our success in learning important lessons from the past makes us very confident about the future. Over the next two decades, we see ourselves having at least five hundred franchises throughout the United States, Canada, the UK, and the Caribbean Community (CARICOM) territories as we become a truly international mega-food chain.

We're a long way from the old Hawthorne & Sons Bakery in Border, but our experiences there prepared us to go all the way in realizing our American Dream.

* * *

Here, finally, are my golden rules, the baker's dozen, little pinches of spice that I either used or learned from my pursuit of success:

1. IDENTIFY YOUR TRUE BUSINESS AND PRODUCT

There can be no entrance into business without a good product. As consumers jostle to get the "best for their bucks," so must the entrepreneur take extra care to ensure the new product will be a win for both consumer and himself. This was the premise on which Golden Krust entered the market: to provide something new but also to gain success doing it. We introduced unique-flavored Jamaican patties and hard dough bread which were basically nonexistent in the American neighborhoods where the Jamaican population resided. After the first few months of entry we knew we had found our niche. This provided the launching pad from which we gradually added items, until we had built the cuisine of our liking. We later complemented this with our look and feel, introducing bright Caribbean sunshiny colors which played a significant role in transporting the minds of our customers to the Caribbean islands.

2. CONDUCT A FEASIBILITY STUDY

Conducting feasibility studies is important to every business. Our early feasibility studies did not have the level of sophistication we enjoy today. We stood on street corners, counted the cars, watched the subways to get an idea of the number of people getting on and off, and we watched their spending patterns and the restaurants they frequented. Our study basically revolved around population, discretionary spending, location, signage, and traffic flow. The information garnered was used to strategically place our Bronx and Brooklyn restaurants near subways and busy thoroughfares.

Today we bask in the sophistication that technology provides, bringing the information we seek to the comfort of our offices. We still believe, however, that nothing beats spending a little time in the location where a new venture will be established. Paying keen attention to this aspect of business for every additional venture undertaken by Golden Krust is one reason we have maintained a very low failure rate.

3. VALUE INTEGRITY CONSISTENTLY

The Golden Krust way of conducting business and the reputation it has earned are etched in the morals engrained in my siblings and me from childhood. Some of these have made their way to our employee and business process manuals and many are unwritten codes of conduct we live by. For me, it's like honoring the guiding principles of integrity, respect, and honesty demonstrated by my parents as they conducted their business and their daily lives. As CEO of Golden Krust, I take on the responsibility to model organizational integrity with the hope of creating a Golden Krust culture where the combined efforts of the staff and management are aligned with our company's values and our commitments to our customers, shareholders, and business partners.

4. RECOGNIZE YOUR EMPLOYEES AS ASSETS

Our first set of employees was me, my siblings, and close relatives who had worked at my parents' bakery in Jamaica. After twenty years in business, nearly everyone who started with us is not only still actively engaged in the business but has grown with us, and now occupy supervisory and management positions. Taking interest in our employees' potential and creating the opportunities for the development of their skills, expertise, and competencies, along with rewarding their efforts, has resulted in tremendous loyalty. Rewarding employees for great work also helps to boost productivity. Additionally, inviting staff input and creativity into the decision-making process stimulates buy-in and a sense of ownership. Managing the company's human resources should be a top priority for every business. Every employee directly or indirectly impacts the growth and development of the business, as well as customer satisfaction. Employees who are made to feel undervalued do little to enhance the well-being of the company.

5. LEAD BY EXAMPLE

Leadership has been defined by some as the "ability to successfully integrate and maximize available resources for the attainment of set goals." Effective leaders are expected to set the example they would like to have employees model and hold true to the values of the organization, ensuring the vision of the company is steadily pursued. As companies grow, many owners make the mistake of becoming too distant from the processes and materials that put their businesses and brands on the map. I still report to work on time and if necessary will work up into the wee hours of the night to ensure that deadlines are met. Insignificant as this may seem, it is my way of instilling good work ethics and boosting morale among our line and management staff, not only by what I say but also by my actions.

6. BE INFORMATION-ORIENTED

Businesses must evolve with the times. One way to ensure

this is to keep abreast of new technologies, methodologies, products, and techniques. Doing this will ensure the business gets the edge over the competition. Thanks to technology, the world is a much smaller place. Brick-and-mortar are no longer necessary for informational meetings and seminars. There has also been an increase in the number of shows, conventions, and expos where businesses have the opportunity to showcase their products; Golden Krust has benefited greatly by its participation and exposure. Introducing a unique restaurant concept that is easily replicated also required us to have a good training program for our franchise owners. Coupled with this is the ongoing training program developed for our staff. Training serves two purposes: to raise the level of efficiency and to assure the employee and/or franchise owner that the company cares about their well-being and success. Business owners cannot become complacent and must continually seek to find how their business can be improved with added knowledge. Failure to do this will be a recipe for failure.

7. Network, Network, Network!

Having good business intelligence doesn't only come from facts; it often comes from your human connections as well. Our expansion and community involvement have gone hand in hand with widespread social and political connections, which combine to give the company a powerful information base. One of the main benefits of this kind of connectedness is that it allows you to know what's going on in political and public circles, making you better able to tap into key information that can result in strategic decision-making. Never part company without sharing your contact information. Always have your business cards on hand.

8. Be a Marketing-Driven Organization

One of the key elements of success in any business is its ability to respond to its customers. The market-driven organization operates with a level of awareness and flexibility which allows it to respond to the changing needs of its customers effectively. The market-driven organization, in striving to remain relevant, must never lose sight of its competitors; through strategic marketing initiatives it must confidently and expertly position itself in the marketplace as a better choice.

One of Golden Krust's key success factors has been its capability to respond quickly to changes, whether environmental or otherwise, and to embrace the risk involved with responding to its customers' needs: at the right time, with the right product or right alternative, and at the right price. A few years ago, our signature items were beef and chicken patties, along with our hard dough white bread. As consumers' tastes and preferences changed and as they became increasingly health conscious, we responded by introducing a vegetable patty, followed by a vegan patty, and complemented that offering with our sumptuous wheat bread and most recently the addition of whole wheat crust for many of our products. Our response to the demand for healthier choices was rapid because we were prepared for them—technologically, logistically, and otherwise. We are always planning ahead. After all, the one thing the consumer consistently seeks is value. The company which is able to deliver the entire package will most definitely be a winner.

9. Endeavor to Become a Good Corporate Citizen

A successful man can never be one with a tight fist. A tight fist lets nothing out but is also incapable of getting much more than what's already in its grasp. The attitude of giving back is a part of the culture of Golden Krust and a memorial to my parents, who instilled this value in me from childhood. It's my belief that a good corporate citizen ensures that the decisions taken are not lopsided but encompass economic, social, and environmental considerations. Not only should plans be based on these considerations, but they should be revealed when the plans are implemented. As a corporate citizen, Golden Krust ensures its manufacturing facility operates under strict best-practices guidelines and environmentally friendly procedures, including proper waste management and recycling efforts.

The company is also well known in the areas it serves for its local partnerships and community participation. Golden Krust continues to inspire and educate those in its reach through scholarships, internships, participation in business development seminars, and dialogue with schools. Our work in the community has not only created customer and employee loyalty, it has also played a major role in our branding.

10. REINVEST IN YOUR BUSINESS

Remaining comfortable is not an option for a company which plans for longevity in business or one which plans to expand, increase resources, or capitalize on market opportunities that might pass to its competitors. Many companies make the mistake of issuing early profit sharing to shareholders before consideration is given to growth strategies. The first few years of a business are usually the slowest, profit may not be at the anticipated level, and frustration may set in, but this should not overshadow the need to reinvest funds in promotional and advertising programs, research and development, and infrastructure.

Reinvestment has been Golden Krust's survival strategy through the years. The company would have lost the opportunities to become part of the growing retail market if it had not redirected a large share of its profit into new machinery, equipment, technology, key personnel, and land acquisition.

11. Strike the Perfect Balance

The daily grind of the business world will sap your passion if you let it. One of the personal challenges of business owners is learning how to keep the passion for business going while striking a balance between business, family, and social engagements. Like many things in life, your passion will ebb and flow depending on the health of your business and whether your risks have paid off and your expectations have been met. Managing the day-to-day operation can also be tiresome and can result in burnout. Breaks bring out the innovative you and rekindle the entrepreneurial flame. The most daring of the decisions I have made—whether investing in real estate, revealing a huge expansion plan, or lobbying the city or state—have been on those days I've taken a break from the office. Not all the innovative ideas are brought to fruition this way, but time off does accomplish the job of refueling.

12. Offer Excellent Customer Service

Exceeding the customer's expectation should be the goal of every business. Businesses must strive to build loyalty. Repeat customers are not only the key to success but an indication of whether the business will fail or survive. A customer is usually disappointed only once, and will turn away from any business which does not deliver the value or experience he/she seeks. The power of "word of mouth" advertising has long been touted as an effective method of promotion. A customer who has a lousy encounter will do as much to publicize this as the one who has a great experience.

13. INVEST IN HUMAN CAPITAL
1) Establish an effective board of directors to help you plan the growth of the company.
2) Take frequent trips and hire people to whom you can delegate some of your responsibilities.
3) Invest in education and training. Investment in training and education does not only motivate, but also improves the morale of your labor force and creates the competitive advantage your business needs.
4) With your extra time, you can focus on your strengths and maximize your capabilities within the parameters you have set for yourself.